PULSE OF THE JUNGLE

DANIEL CLELAND

PULSE OF THE JUNGLE

AYAHUASCA, ADVENTURES, AND SOCIAL ENTERPRISE IN THE AMAZON

PULSE OF THE JUNGLE

Ayahuasca, Adventures, and
Social Enterprise in the Amazon

ISBN   978-1-61961-516-8   *Paperback*

978-1-61961-517-5   *Ebook*

LIONCREST
PUBLISHING

This book is dedicated to the rule breakers, the trailblazers, and the nonconformists of the world. We need you now more than ever. Your value is in your ability to refuse, to persist, and to drive change in the world. As humanity navigates the most important time in history, you will rise as the innovators and thought leaders we need to survive and to thrive well into the future.

CONTENTS

"The reasonable man adapts himself to the world; the unreasonable one persists in trying to adapt the world to himself. Therefore all progress depends on the unreasonable man."

GEORGE BERNARD SHAW

INTRODUCTION

USUALLY, WHEN PEOPLE SAY THEY HIT "ROCK bottom," they mean it metaphorically. In my case, it was literal.

It was November 27, 2009, and there I was, one Canadian man flat on his back at the bottom of a cliff by the Brisbane River. I had come to Australia to further my education, enjoy an adventure, make some money, and maybe even fall in love. None of that was working out as planned. I was out of school, out of work, out of everything except maybe the capacity to make dubious decisions fueled by my ever-growing sense of despair.

That's how I found myself climbing a twenty-meter cliff in the middle of the night. Alone. In dress shoes.

Needless to say, the climb didn't turn out the way I had

pictured it either. One missed grip sent me falling straight down to the ground below, where I lay with a broken leg and busted pelvis. It was the worst night of my life.

The great thing about hitting the bottom, though, is that there is no way to go but up. During my month-long hospital stay, I had a lot of time to think about what "up" might look like. One idea I kept coming back to was using ayahuasca for healing and growth. I had read a lot about the South American plant medicine, but now, life circumstances made me determined to try it. I needed to turn things around.

I had no idea at the time, but my accident—along with the challenges that came before and after—was a valuable part of my journey from lost college student to successful social entrepreneur. When I look back on it now, I see that there really were no mistakes along the way, no matter how rough the route was at the time.

I've written this book to help you create the road to your dream life, no matter how many setbacks or obstacles you may encounter. I hope that by reading my story, you will see that it is possible to get your heart's desire if you persevere.

This book tells the story of how I followed the threads of my interests and managed to turn them into a viable social enterprise—Pulse Tours and Ayahuasca Adventure Center—by successfully navigating challenges and engaging with others who shared my vision.

Pulse Tours is a spiritual adventure company operating in South American countries such as Peru, Colombia, and Brazil. Ayahuasca Adventure Center is a spiritual healing center located at the 2.2 million hectare Pacaya-Samiria reserve near Iquitos, Peru, where you can actually feel the air pulsing with plant, animal, and human life.

This book, however, is not only about what we do at Pulse. It's about how we got there, and how other people can get there, too. Our work with traditional spiritual practices, consciousness-expanding plant medicines, health and fitness, and intercultural exploration can be part of that journey. However, what I'm most interested in is showing people that getting out of their comfort zone, breaking through cultural limitations, following their passions, and making a positive impact on people and planet can bring happiness in a way that money or possessions or relationships simply won't.

I will show you that it is entirely possible to create an amazing life and/or business that fulfills your dreams and changes the world in one. With some sacrifices, dedication, and hard work, you can make your desires a reality. My hope is that my story will educate and inspire you to embark on your own life-changing adventure.

PART ONE

—

SPARK

CHAPTER ONE

FINDING GOLD

CLIMBING OUT OF THE HOLE I'D DUG FOR MYSELF in Australia meant finding my own way in the dark. My body was healing, but my soul was still in turmoil. I was starting to see how experiencing an authentic ayahuasca retreat in the Amazon jungle might spark the inner-healing process I so badly needed. It took years for me to make my way to Peru; by then, I was fascinated with shamanic ideology and ready for the mystical adventure to begin. I had "taste tested" ayahuasca in New Mexico—more on that later—but Peru would offer a much richer experience.

By February 2011, I was in the Amazon. I traveled the chewed-up gravel streets of Puerto Maldonado—thick with sputtering two-stroke engines and kiosks offering pirated goods—into the trees. As the roads got rougher, the scenery got greener. Arriving at the Shimbre Shamanic Center, I thought, *This is the rain forest.*

It was impossible to not feel completely at peace. Against the backdrop of endless miles of Amazon rain forest, the hilltop property was neatly manicured, though chickens scavenged confidently among a handful of playful dogs. The central ceremonial structure, the maloca, was more imposing than I had imagined from photos. The balmy air held the sweet, thick aroma of moist vegetation.

That first taste of ayahuasca in New Mexico had gotten my attention, but this was a whole new level of commitment. Here, I would experience an authentic ayahuasca retreat in the plant medicine's native home. I was still quite a novice and extremely nervous about what was set to transpire. I was excited but scared, too. Although I was convinced that I was doing the right thing, I thought more than once about backing out. In fact, I probably had that moment of doubt for the first twenty ceremonies I did. Participating in an ayahuasca ceremony can be a grueling process; you can't predict what you might face physically, emotionally, and spiritually.

THINGS GET REAL

The maloca was set up like a royal structure, a round building high up on a great concrete platform. Screen walls let us see out over the swath of rain forest and swampland that led to the river. Stairs offered a path down into the jungle below. At about four or five in the afternoon, the shaman initiated the ceremony, gathering our group in the maloca. At that time of day in the Amazon, so close to the equator, the sun goes down at about six o'clock in the evening. By five o'clock, we were surrounded by the hazy, orange-and-pink glow of sunset.

The shaman's entrance reinforced the mystical feeling. He came out dressed in the traditional clothing of the Chavin people, the earliest artists and architects of the Andes, known for their elaborately designed temples. In his hands, the shaman carried a hand-carved scepter and some rattles. His clothing set him apart from the participants, who were clearly his students, not his peers. He was a short, chubby man with a big potbelly, and he was not interested in sharing social niceties. From his spot at the rear of the maloca, he looked out at all of us sitting in rows on either side in chairs.

Traditional songs and dancing launched the ceremony. The shaman shook his rattles, whistled with his eyes closed, and chanted to summon the spirits of the medicine. After about thirty minutes, he handed me a coffee cup full of ayahuasca. I have to admit, it looked revolting. And there was so much of it! In my one earlier ceremony in New Mexico, I had taken a concentrated syrup out of a shot glass, but this was a watery brew that filled a large coffee cup almost to overflowing. My stomach started to turn just looking at it.

Once served, I learned that I was not to drink it on the spot, but to take it down to a hut in the jungle below. To get there, I had to walk down a very steep, winding staircase built into the side of the hill. I carefully navigated seventy-five stairs down a nearly vertical slope to reach the swampy forest floor paths that led to my cabin. Boardwalks covered the worst of the water, though many of those were rotten and broke when I stepped on them.

At this point, I was essentially on my own. Each participant stayed in one of twenty-seven or twenty-eight huts set away from the others on tiny trails that ran into the jungle. It was a bit of a labyrinth and somewhat complicated to navigate during the day, let alone at night. It was still daylight at this point, though the sun was nearly setting. I made my way to my hut and got settled in with blankets and a small foam mattress. I had my purge bucket by my side because a common effect of ayahuasca is a cleansing purge, most frequently by vomiting.

I scattered around some personal artifacts I carried with me, including good luck charms, stones I had collected from different countries, crystals my sister had given me, and a small, handwoven Shipibo tapestry. My friend Bahu had given me this last item, telling me that the Shipibo Indians of the Amazon jungle were the stewards of ayahuasca medicine.

I began to realize the profound nature of my undertaking. I was sitting there, about to drink the medicine, knowing it could take me off to a challenging place. It might be a beautiful journey or a terrifying one. I took a moment to ground myself in my surroundings. I was in the Amazon jungle for the first time, huddled in my hut, surrounded by forest. I was ready.

I slammed back that coffee cup of ayahuasca like I would a glass of beer. There was no sipping or tasting. It was just bottoms up. I lay down on my mat and awaited the effects.

When the effects came, they were overwhelming. I had little context for this experience, but in retrospect I can say that it was one of the hardest ceremonies I've ever had, not just on a mental level but physically, too. I wasn't prepared for navigating the physical world while I was fully under the influence of the medicine.

WIDE OPEN

I felt the medicine's power skyrocket only ten or fifteen minutes after drinking it. Within an hour, it had taken full control. I cannot accurately describe the worlds I entered, lying on the floor of my hut with my eyes open. The clear sky allowed the full moon to shine down through the trees and illuminate the tangled, gnarly roots and jungle foliage that surrounded me.

When I closed my eyes, I witnessed an alternate dimension of indescribable beauty. Bright colors and geometrical designs shifted before me. Unblinking eyes gazed benevolently at me, signifying a realm of universal intelligence. I heard a voice repeatedly saying to me, "Welcome."

I was shown a corridor through which I was invited to walk.

A canine figure, perhaps a coyote, appeared in front of me. He was fully alert and stared down the corridor with a curious look, ears perked, and eyes focused. He was not afraid but moved cautiously ahead. After a couple of steps forward, he would sit back on his haunches and observe. I was not confident enough to follow just yet.

As the visions came and went, my motor skills deteriorated. I entered a different space where a child stood holding out his hand to me. Again, I heard him say, "Welcome." I was in some otherworldly version of a jungle, more pristine and peaceful than any on earth.

This was ayahuasca's realm. Long vines hung down in tight, stringy coils. Clear water ran softly below the structure that supported us. I felt nausea building, but the ayahuasca would not let go so quickly. The sounds of the jungle—frogs, insects, strange things I couldn't explain—intensified as the bright moon rose higher in the sky.

My thoughts turned to my family. I could see them all: my sisters, my mother, my father, my grandparents, cousins, aunts, and uncles. Feeling a profound sense of love and gratitude, I wanted to share this experience with them.

The turbulence in my digestive tract had reached an

uncomfortable threshold at this point, and I hunched over my bucket hoping to expel the unpleasant sensation in my stomach. My intestines began to bubble, a concerning signal that tonight the purge would be coming from both ends. I tried to locate the door, thinking of toilets and tissue paper that lay at the other end of the winding jungle trails, but my vision was impaired dramatically and the unrest in my stomach forced me to suspend my face above the purge bucket on hands and knees.

All the while, my visions continued unabated. Even with my eyes open, I had graphic scenes playing out before me, with sexually attractive, scantily clothed female bodies standing in my direct line of sight. I was amazed by the intricacy and beauty I witnessed. Still, the nausea surged, and I pulled the bucket even closer.

My mouth was so dry—the shaman's rules forbade drinking water or eating food the day of the ceremony—I couldn't imagine passing the acidic contents that now swirled around my stomach through it, but I had no choice. Without a trace of dignity, I unloaded the searing liquid into the bucket and felt the most immense sense of release and relief.

Exhausted from holding my pose above the bucket, I flopped down on the floor mat. I breathed deeply, though I could feel that the ordeal wasn't quite over. My intestines continued to churn; I needed to find a toilet. I had two choices; I either had to coordinate my rubbery muscles and brace myself over the purge bucket in my hut or brave the swarm of bloodthirsty Amazon mosquitoes that lay in wait outside the door. Neither option was attractive, but I couldn't just soil myself inside my hut.

My only acceptable option became clear. I had to get to the toilets at the top of the trail. Peeling myself off the floor, I managed to raise myself to standing. My legs wobbled and my perception was unreliable. I made my move, opening the door, feeling my way down the stairs and commencing the walk onto the trail leading to the property above.

The trail quickly grew darker, concealing the path behind me. There was no going back. I had left my flashlight in the hut; I had no choice but to keep moving forward. Slowly, I edged one foot out in front of the other, grasping for whatever handrail I could find. My slow pace made the trail seem infinitely longer than I remembered. Could I have gone in the wrong direction? I couldn't tell. There were dogs barking above, but I couldn't distinguish from which direction.

I may have been going the wrong way, but I found a step. If I could only follow the steps, I knew I would make it to the top. Endlessly, it seemed, I climbed every tedious, tiring step. Step, step, step, and finally, there it was, a solemn glimmer of moonlight beaming down through the opening in the top of the stairway. I was nearing the top.

When I caught sight of the giant ceremonial structure,

I was so relieved. Now I just needed to traverse the dark trails across the property. I had walked them countless times and was relatively confident I could find my way to the Holy Grail: a white building with double bathrooms. There it was.

Of course the light switch didn't produce any light. I could barely see the empty roll that hung from the toilet tissue dispenser. The water tap produced nothing but a momentary gasp of air. Next door in the other bathroom I found the same situation.

At this point, I wondered if the shaman had turned off the water on purpose, if only to intensify the challenge. After all, that is one of the objectives of this work.

Exhausted and frustrated, I walked back to my room to lie down. The visual effects of the ayahuasca were still strong. Energetic trails of light and energy lagged behind my fingers as I moved my hands. I marveled at the motion of the light trails, but nothing could distract me from the fact that I had no water, I was desperately thirsty, and I still needed a toilet badly.

First, I tried to sleep, but the ayahuasca kept me awake. Somewhere around eleven o'clock, I realized there was no way I was going to be able to wait until the bathrooms were sorted out in the morning. I remembered another set of toilets I had seen the day before in front of a different cabin. I was forced to once again venture onto the trail system in the dark but was able to find two older structures with toilets. Again, I found no lights and no toilet paper, but one thing I did have was running water sourced from a rainwater catchment tank, rather than the main spring. My relief was overwhelming, and I was finally able to relax and return to the comfort and security of my bed for a good night's rest.

AFTERSHOCKS

When I woke up, I felt that I had just undergone a training exercise. It tested my mental resilience, strength of will, and independence. It put into perspective life's more mundane challenges, things we often place too much emphasis on. Here, I could see that we are equipped to handle so much more. I was proud of myself for overcoming the struggle.

My first Amazon ayahuasca ceremony gave me a profound spiritual experience. Regular perception was pushed to its limits so that I was forced to consider the existence of a supernatural energy or entity. I'm not necessarily suggesting this was God but rather, a divine presence.

A welcome aftereffect of a ceremony like this is the feeling of lightness that comes from a significant purge. My insides felt clean from top to bottom. I felt like I had eliminated stuff that had been stuck inside me, physically and psychologically.

THE WHOLE PICTURE

When I look back now, after years of running similar

retreats for others, I can see that I was just beginning to explore the seeds of what would become my life's work. At the time, though, I didn't realize any of that. My thoughts were much more immediate. I wanted to explore my own limits, to investigate the boundaries of the universe. I needed to know if there was some type of higher existence I could reach by journeying through my own psyche. These plants offered the promise of experiencing a superior level of reality, perhaps a hint of what waits for us in death. I was interested in separating consciousness from ego and even destroying the ego for a moment in time.

I felt called to go deeper. I realized that all people should be able to have this experience. Being able to go to this place, this realm away from ego and memory, is an important part of being human. The shift in perspective offered by ayahuasca lets you see life as pure consciousness.

Some people expect an ayahuasca experience to help them find a new world, but to me, it was more about experiencing all aspects of the world that already exist. It was like uncovering a reality that has been there all along; you simply haven't been properly equipped to see it.

What ayahuasca allows is something like taking an electron microscope and looking into the quantum movement of electrons in atoms. That stuff is there all along, whether you can perceive it or not. Everything is made up of these vibrating ions and particles, but you don't see it unless you look for it specifically and unless you have a tool that can illuminate that scale of existence. Ayahuasca can be such a tool.

One of the active constituents in ayahuasca, dimethyltryptamine (DMT), creates this channel into a new way of perceiving. People often describe their experience of DMT, when consumed as an extract, in a very similar way. Most encounter spirit, God, the divine, or extraterrestrial intelligence. Many travel with their consciousness into the center of the universe and come to understand how the universe functions at the energetic level. They recognize the order and motive of everything we perceive to exist.

This world is always there. You just need to cut through the vines of your ego and your human perception in order to see it. There's nothing inherently wrong with being human, but the human experience is incredibly enhanced by having knowledge of something greater.

I confess that even with all of the obvious benefits, I was pretty intimidated to continue with the retreat. At this point I was still a very entry-level participant in the world of ayahuasca. I was thrilled to have survived my first Amazon ayahuasca experience, but I knew it was just the tip of the iceberg compared to what could happen if I continued.

REACHING BEYOND SELF

Before we go much further in my personal journey, we should explore more about how Pulse Tours and Ayahuasca Adventure Center came to be.

My first authentic ayahuasca experience was transformative for me, and I could see how life-changing it was for the other participants as well. I knew I wanted to make this paradigm shift available for others. As it turned out, one of the most satisfying aspects of running our ayahuasca adventure center in Peru is seeing people come in seeking healing they haven't been able to get anywhere else and witnessing their connection with the medicine. Sometimes participants will write to me after their stay, sharing that they've had an incredible encounter and achieved something they couldn't even imagine. Even though they don't really know me, they feel like they know me just by being at the place that I designed with heart and soul. When I get those messages, it makes enduring all of the uncertainty and challenge of entrepreneurship that much more worthwhile.

The center took shape over a number of years, with the help of my teammates, particularly my fiancée, Tatyana Telegina, who now runs the center with me. The seeds were planted back in that hospital room in Australia, but momentum really took hold in 2012, when I led an adventure into the Amazon to have an ayahuasca ceremony for the infamous "end of the world" date of December 21, 2012. We traveled from Bogotá, Colombia, to the city of Iquitos, Peru, where I had experienced my first ayahuasca ceremonies under the Shipibo tradition.

Iquitos is one of the main hot spots for jungle tourism. People come to Iquitos and work with agencies that set them up with guides who take them through pristine jungle parks such as the Pacaya-Samiria Nature Reserve. It's a great spot for jungle tours, so there are a number of jungle lodges throughout the area.

From the beginning, our programs mixed jungle tours and adventure with ayahuasca, though not integrated into the same day. We would go on a jungle tour, then do a four- or five-day ayahuasca retreat at someone else's center. While staying at other ayahuasca retreat centers, our passengers spent a lot of time lying in hammocks, meditating, playing cards, and writing in their journals, but there wasn't a lot of activity after the ceremonies. (Our guests are often referred to as "passengers" because of the physical and mental journeys they take.) The participants weren't exercising; everything was stationary. I had a feeling we could do more with this time.

By 2014, although we had some success working with other centers, we were scrambling to grow our own operation. Tatyana hadn't held a job since we met, and I had given up my job with the intention of taking what was then called just Pulse Tours to a new level—a full-time business—that would sustain us. We were getting busier and busier, and receiving rave reviews online.

Meanwhile, I was trying to negotiate a deal with one center to give us more availability and better prices; we were having trouble taking the regular price and putting a markup on it and then selling it. We were bringing a lot of business to the center, so I made a deal with one of the owners, agreeing to invest in building some extra cabins at their other property, near a maloca that was already built but not in use.

The plan was that we would bring our groups there and use the cabins I had invested in, while their shamans would conduct ceremonies for us in this one special, smaller maloca. It seemed like it would work well. A handshake and an ayahuasca ceremony would seal the deal—or so I thought. Unfortunately, during that night's ceremony, the owner meditated on the deal and realized it was not going to work out after all. We were back to square one. That's when I knew we were done working at the mercy of other people's decisions when it came to our business.

We quickly realized we needed to build our own place, where we could play by our own rules. Once that decision was made, we had a ceremony where I visualized the operation. I received an image of the big sky at Libertad, a tiny native village near the Pacaya-Samiria National Reserve, where we had already guided a number of jungle adventures. It's on a wide-open river, and you can see the whole sky. Libertad was so unlike the inland retreat centers where we'd been working under a jungle canopy that blocked the sky and felt claustrophobic.

I conceptualized an ayahuasca center that was more active, a little less somber, and a lot more fun than many of the other centers. I didn't want everyone to just be sitting around. Instead, we would integrate the adventure of travel and the jungle environment into the whole experience. People would be traveling across the world to encounter this powerful psychedelic medicine that would take them into the deepest parts of their psyches and show them the infinite fabric of the universe. That's an adventure! So many places we went to were very serious and took the fun out of it. The Pulse experience would be different. We were going to make it a jungle adventure and an ayahuasca healing experience all in one.

It made sense from a biological perspective. People were coming down to detox, to purge. Exercise—sweating, boosting your heart rate, and burning fat—could only add to the purification. On top of that, participants would get the well-known benefit of being in nature, interacting with animals, and breathing clean air. Scientifically, it followed that we should put it all together.

We took a little flak for calling our place an "adventure center" because the accepted practice in ayahuasca circles was to maintain a very serious, solemn atmosphere. Our passengers, however, are already very knowledgeable about the traditions; they understand where the medicine comes from. They want more. One early passenger gave us the feedback we needed to reaffirm that "adventure" would be a core concept for us. After her time with us, she said the active nature of the retreat was a valuable part of her experience. We knew, too, a more celebratory approach would help differentiate us from others.

Another way we stood out was by integrating a gym into our facilities. One of my pet peeves about other centers was that you couldn't stay fit. You would stay there and waste away on the skimpy food and lack of activity. I designed our site to include a gym from the beginning.

Our vision of an integrated experience also included animals; we have several animals living at the center. Everybody loves the playful antics of Martina, our woolly monkey, and cheeky little Ricardo, a rescued pygmy marmoset. Greeting all our guests with gusto is our dog, Raffa, and our cats, sisters Ayahuasca and Chacruna. I wanted that welcoming vibe, where everyone smiles and treats each other with love and respect, so we added multicolored hammocks, artwork on the walls, and a library.

Some of my early experiences had been less than ideal, so I wanted our center to be different. I had been through ceremonies that were preceded by difficult fasts—a practice considered legitimate in most Shipibo traditions—but I wasn't convinced it was necessary to such a degree, for the average bear. Nor was the no-sugar, no-salt ayahuasca diet often prescribed. I tested the effects of diet myself one night while I was at Shimbre Shamanic Center in 2011, eating pork and having a beer before a ceremony, and that night I had an incredibly powerful ceremony. I had also been to ceremonies in Brazil with the Santo

Daime and União do Vegetal (UDV) religions that featured a huge feast before the ceremony, so I knew the fasting rule wasn't written in stone. Although, I have to say I do not recommend eating pork or drinking beer before ceremonies!

I wanted people to feel nourished and safe, even as we asked them to take risks and expand their boundaries through ayahuasca and adventure. My role is a little bit like the coyote figure in Native American mythology: I meet people at the edge of their comfort zone and playfully coax them into a new world.

One thing I wanted to avoid was turning newcomers off from the experience simply because the preparation was unnecessarily harsh. That's what happened when my father agreed to try ayahuasca. I had lobbied long and hard for him to experience what I was experiencing. On his sixtieth birthday, he came with my uncle to give it a try. Unfortunately, the center we went to at the time insisted on having participants drink a preceremony purgative plant brew that made them so sick they abandoned their plans to continue. I was incredibly annoyed and vowed to take a different approach at our center.

Some people criticize us for not following protocol. They see it as irresponsible or lacking in respect for the traditions, but I see it as creating traditions based on my own experience, which is broader than most other people in the field. A lot of people have worked a long time in one tradition, but how many have immersed themselves in four different traditions, as I have? My hope is that people will see that I'm open-minded and inquisitive, always investigating things to get at the truth. I never blindly accept what's handed down. Instead, I earn trust by trying things for myself before recommending them to others.

SLOW BUILD

While the development of the Ayahuasca Adventure Center moved swiftly after the 2014 Brazil trip, I definitely took the long way to get there. Going from Canadian college dropout to successful businessman in the jungles of Peru would take a while.

After high school, I tried to enter the working world I saw my father and peers inhabiting, but I couldn't settle on a path. I cycled through four different programs in four years of college. All of them were courses I selected by flipping through pages in a college catalog, expending little effort to understand what the related job might entail. My father was working for a nuclear power plant in the technology sector, and I wanted to find something that would live up to the image I had of what he considered respectable.

Beginning in 2000, I attended Fanshawe College of Arts and Technology in London, Ontario, Canada. I switched from studying computer programming to electronics engineering and eventually cobbled together enough classes to qualify for a certificate in electrical techniques, which I never actually collected. I loved the science, the theories, and design work, but the hands-on technical work was not my forte. One of my teachers actually said to me, "You should not be a technician. You are so full of shit. You should be a salesperson." I had no idea how right he was.

My first job after college was—surprise—a sales job. The position was listed in the paper as an air quality technician, which sounded similar enough to my college programs that I thought I could talk my way through the interview. That I did, but it turned out to be 100-percent sales. I thought the company was cool at first, but it was sleazy. It presented itself as providing a service for homeowners to remove carcinogenic particulate compounds from their indoor air. Its solution was a negative ionizer with an electronic air filter that the lucky homeowner could own for a mere $3,000. The company went line by line through the phone book and called everyone to congratulate them on winning a free vacation if only they would invite us in to deliver the prize, along with a spiel on the air purifier.

For maybe six months, I managed to work the script. I dutifully informed families about the dust mites in their carpet and the evils of indoor air pollution before hauling in the forty-pound purifier that would miraculously pull a visible film of dust through its filter. I would then triumphantly hold up the filter as proof that our machine could clean their air.

I was never very good at pushing people. I probably lost about 20 percent of my sales with that company because I didn't push people as hard as management wanted me to. The straw that broke the camel's back was when I was sent to my hometown to sell these machines. Unbelievably, they wanted me to sell to my grandparents. I couldn't do it. When I realized then that I was selling something I was not comfortable enough to sell to my own loved ones, I quit. No more going into working people's homes and conning them out of their hard-earned money.

Besides, I was interested in moving on to business-to-business sales, so I turned my attention to working my way up through an electrical sales company in Ontario. It was expanding into the oil and gas industry in Alberta. That was a good job for a while. I had a lot of autonomy, and Ontario is a fairly clean, developed area. I wasn't necessarily in touch with how our work was affecting the environment, though.

As an avid follower of David Suzuki and the environmentalist movement and a rural Canadian, I should have been more aware. I grew up in the countryside, reading books like *Call of the Wild* and *White Fang*, spending the days hiking around the forest, starting campfires and cooking on them. As an adult, I continued to spend a lot of time in nature, hiking and connecting to the land.

Eventually, my job took me face to face with what the oil and gas industry was doing to the landscape I loved. I was sent to Fort McMurray in Alberta, home of the Athabasca oil sands. When I first moved to Alberta, I hadn't really noticed anything. I lived in Calgary, where the facilities were small scale. It's not like they had big smoke stacks belching out black smoke. This was Canada. You couldn't just do that, right?

It didn't appear I was doing anything awful for the environment, apart from driving a lot. I remained unconcerned until I had harvested all of the low-hanging sales fruit in Calgary and I had to travel farther to get more contracts. I started driving up to Fort McMurray, where the monster facilities for Petro-Canada, Suncor, and Enbridge were. I had high hopes. This was the big time we had been working toward all along.

What I saw up there, though, was horrifying. From twenty miles away, I could see megalithic smoke stacks bellowing out huge clouds of carbon dioxide and pollution. It looked like they were forming their own clouds. Then I came upon massive open pit mines that were like something out of a nightmare. There was complete destruction of the landscape as far as the eye could see.

I was appalled, and yet I was walking through it all with the maintenance managers and technicians, pretending it wasn't bothering me. I knew, though, that I wanted this whole thing to stop. It disgusted me to think I was becoming one of them, capitalizing on this rampant destruction of the local environment. How could I be party to the toxic waste and tailings that were killing flocks of birds and poisoning the water supply? That's when I started to think about getting out of there, traveling to Brazil and moving on to something else.

My environmental convictions were telling me to move on, but I also had simpler motives familiar to any young man: I wanted to impress a girl—a Swiss girl. She had come to Canada as an exchange student in the late nineties, and I had kept in contact with her over the years. I felt I had never been quite good enough for her. She had traveled the world and helped me recognize the limitations and faults of the cultural bubble that I was conditioned to, the small-town mindset I grew up with. I had the idea that a solo adventure in Brazil would prove to her that I had broken out of my provincial perspective. The trip didn't play out romantically the way I wanted, but it did get me to step outside that bubble in a big way.

Brazil was also the home country of Sepultura, one of my favorite heavy metal bands at the time. Their music was so raw and tribal sounding that it felt like a perfect fit with my personality. I loved hot weather, and I wanted awesome beaches, hot ladies, and good music. Brazil promised all this with the exotic addition of a rain forest adventure. I was so excited.

I booked my trip over Christmas and New Year's,

when it's freezing in Canada but toasty on the beach in Copacabana. It was a blast. I spent time in a hostel and got to know some guys from the Netherlands, Australia, and England. I just traveled at will for a couple of weeks. Back in Copacabana for New Year's Eve, I was offered a bartending job at the hostel.

The fates were smiling on me. Not only did I have a job, I seemed to have a magic wand where the ladies were concerned and exactly the lifestyle I wanted. I would wake up and walk or run down the beach, getting a suntan while exercising in these handy outdoor gyms along the way. I felt free.

Technically, I was only free for six weeks, until my boss back in Canada expected me back. I really did not want to go back. I had a good friend, Henry, and a beautiful new love interest, Renata. But I had to go. On the way to the airport, I cracked. I shed a few tears, telling the driver that "leaving Brazil is like pulling the heart out of my chest." He knew just what I meant and replied, "Well, I guess you know where to come when you want to find your heart again."

When I got back to Calgary, I was just done. Done with winter, done with driving seven hours up to Fort McMurray for appointments with these massive polluters—everything. I was obsessed with Brazil and started researching outfits that offered tours there. I had talked with some of those tour companies a few years earlier, but now I had experience with travel and foreign languages.

I threw together a résumé and ended up getting a job with what was then called G.A.P. Adventures, (now called G Adventures). Guides and tour leaders had to be fluent in Spanish and Portuguese, so I leveraged my previous trips to Spain, Mexico, and Brazil, which helped a lot. My sales skills came into play as well; I knew how to converse and deal with customers. I really sold myself in the interview process and within a couple of months began a training program in Central America.

Training was thorough. In spring 2007, I flew down for a two-week course that took us from Guatemala to Mexico, then to Belize. During the trip, we were put in real-life situations where we had to accomplish challenging objectives in strange, new places. They also taught us about business operations, how to maintain a budget, and how to deal with difficult passengers. We practiced all of the skills needed to be in charge of fifteen people traveling from place to place in a developing country.

My first assignment was in Costa Rica and Panama, beginning with a fifteen-day trip. We launched from San Jose, Costa Rica, and went to Puerto Viejo before crossing the border into Panama. We followed the Bocas del Toro Archipelago and continued up into the mountains of El Valle and then on to Panama City. Once in Panama City, I would say good-bye to that group of people, pick up another group, and do the reverse route.

When that first tour kicked off, I was thrilled. I had a

great crew of people, some from Scotland, the United States, Canada, and Singapore. I made an event out of my initiation as a tour leader with a contest. Whoever won got to shave my head, so I had a Mohawk hairstyle for a little while.

I struggled with Spanish at first, but it slowly improved. I ran the Panama experience five or six times, plus a bunch of hiking, biking, and rafting tours, which were my favorite. We'd take off on a three-day hike high up into the jungle and stay in rustic cabins in the rain forest of the Caribbean near Limón. It got messy in the rainy season, but the trips were fantastic, including white water rafting and some pretty intense mountain biking up in the Arenal Volcano.

Out in the wilderness like this, I was having the time of my life. I did run into some trouble in Panama City, though, when half of our group went to one bar and half to another, leaving me walking down the sidewalk alone, not particularly sober myself. From out of nowhere, I was attacked by a local man. He took offense to my attitude, I guess. I remember him saying, "Well, you think you can just walk through our country and do whatever you want?" I probably made some smartass comment in return, and things escalated pretty quickly.

Soon, I was a bloody mess, and we were both hauled off to the police station for the night. Sometime the next morning, the cops took us to the local "courthouse," which was a tiny room off a hot, dodgy street where we sat on card table chairs for hours, sweating and bleeding. Several young military guys sat there staring at us with their hands on their pistols. They were dressed in olive green military suits, so they looked official, but the room was very strange. One of the walls was stacked from floor to ceiling with crates of empty beer bottles. In this dubious setting, the "court" proceedings unfolded. We pleaded our stories, and it was ruled that my attacker would have to pay for me to get my face fixed. It was all so surreal.

Meanwhile, my tour group was back in their hotel rooms, wondering what had happened to me. The last they had seen, I was walking away with the police, with a paper towel stuck to my face and blood running everywhere. We had a tour to Isla Taboga planned for the next day.

Plans would have to change because I needed to get my nose put back in place. The options ranged from the expensive (time-consuming surgery by a legitimate doctor in a clean operating room with proper anesthesia) to the fast fix (find a guy who for $100 would stick a couple of metal rods up my nose and bust it back into place). Of course I chose the latter.

Then I was on my way back to Canada, where I had to greet my parents with a cast on my nose and two black eyes. I also weighed about ten kilograms less than when I had left. I told my dad the whole story, and he just looked at me and said, "Huh. Sounds like you were talking when you should've been listening."

Right as he was, I was undeterred and ready to go back.

OUT OF THE FRYING PAN, INTO THE FIRE

I ended up leading tours in Costa Rica and Panama until December 2007. That's when I got notice I was being transferred to South America. My first tour there was long, a forty-two-day trip that started in Caracas, Venezuela, and coursed over to the Caribbean side to a town called Santa Fe. From there, we went directly south, stopping in Ciudad Bolívar, where we would do a tour of the Canaima National Park, Angel Falls, and the Grand Savannah. Continuing on, we visited Santa Elena, and then crossed the border into Brazil and eventually made our way by road down to Manaus. Then we were off on a jungle tour in Manaus followed by a five-day boat ride down the Amazon River to a city called Belém. We weren't done yet. Next, we traced the Brazilian coastline down to Salvador da Bahia. From Salvador, we would take a flight to Rio de Janeiro to complete the trip.

My first group had eight people, seven women and one man. That might have seemed like a lucky break for me at first, but it didn't turn out that way. None of the ladies got along, and they ranged in age from eighteen to midsixties. They were all from different worlds, from the twenty-four-year-old ex-model who exuded cool to the two gentile old friends in their sixties.

Aside from the social interactions, logistics became a nightmare. Sleeping arrangements were tricky. There was an odd number of women and just one man, and he was not the best match for the group. Any other guy might have been fine, but this Australian man was fairly crude, coming from an all-boys boarding school background and having worked in the mines in western Australia. He was constantly rude to the women, who couldn't stand him.

Usually when I was leading tours, I'd be able to get my own room and have a little space to myself. Not this time, though. It felt like we were together 24-7 for the entire six weeks, like we were on the *Big Brother* television show or something.

I gamely got us started, however, just before Christmas, traveling from Caracas straight to Santa Fe. It was my first time there. Santa Fe is a small Caribbean town—not Caribbean in the stereotypical sense, but it's on the Caribbean Sea, so it's hot and sunny, a bit rough, and a little trashy.

If I'd entertained any thoughts about Christmas being an auspicious time to launch this journey, they were quickly dispelled by the events of December 24, 2007. Our group was strolling single-file through the sandy little town in the middle of the day, in sight of the police station, no less, when a barefoot kid came charging out of one of the alleyways with a gun in his hand. One of the women carried a big film camera on a lanyard strapped around her neck, and this kid grabbed it, trying to rip it off her. Her screams reached me at the front of the line. I ran to help, but this kid saw me coming a mile away.

He pointed his gun at me, and I was like, "Yeah, no

thanks. You can have the camera." He had taken it off the woman's neck by then and dashed back into the alley, prize in hand. We reported it to the police, but they didn't seem concerned at all, even though it happened practically outside their police station.

That was the start of an uncomfortable six weeks. I felt underqualified for the journey because the territory was new to me and very remote. We ran into lots of crime, black market currency conversions, and armed criminals. It was a really rough-and-tumble country, overwhelming to negotiate with a group of cranky travelers gossiping and fighting the whole time.

Nonetheless, we finished the journey in Rio, landing there just in time for Carnival. The party atmosphere offered a reward for a year of hard work, biding my circumstances, creating opportunities, and following through with presence and determination. I had started with a goal in mind—get back to Brazil—and here I was.

Instead of focusing solely on my own experience, though, I'd like to introduce some other people who have come to ayahuasca and found themselves transformed by the experience. I will share several such stories in people's own words throughout the book.

STORIES OF PERSONAL TRANSFORMATION: JOLÉ FOY

Artist and designer Jolé Foy has done almost twenty ceremonies with Pulse Tours and Ayahuasca Adventure Center. She has grown from a place of uncertainty and illness to create a vibrant life and business making transcendent silver and stone jewelry in her own studio and selling it around the world. She sells her work online through Lavender Star Designs.

"[When] I started looking into [ayahuasca], I found Tatyana [Tatyana Telegina is cofounder of the Pulse Tours and Ayahuasca Adventure Center] online. I ended up talking to her for about a year before I actually went to Pulse for the first time. The first time I went there was May of last year [2015]. I was dealing with things that most people do...traumas...and I was suppressing my emotions and lashing out in anger. Just wasn't very centered or anything like that.

"I did four ceremonies the first time. It was amazing. I learned to love myself, which I don't think I've ever done before. I also uncovered some trauma that I wasn't aware of, so I went back a second time. After coming home the first time, I felt more aware of myself and I started trusting my intuition.

"I decided to start trying different things. I tried silversmithing and I fell in love with it. I kind of had a feeling that it was something I needed to pursue, so I bought all of the tools and I read every book I could find and watched every tutorial. I built a studio in my home and I pretty much locked myself in and taught myself how to silversmith.

"[I had done] beading and simple stuff like that but nothing that's near as involved as this. I went back again to Pulse for three weeks in January of this year [2016]. I had visions. [During] one ceremony, she [ayahuasca is often spoken of as a feminine presence] showed me my hands and she showed me the strength and dexterity and talents in them. The experience reaffirmed that that's what I'm supposed to be doing. I came home and in March I quit my job of ten years to design full time. It was the best decision I've ever made. It's amazing to stay home all day and create beautiful things and people love it. I feel really lucky.

"Personally, I was emotionally shut off before and now I'm very aware of my feelings and I'm able to process emotions. I'm more open to other people. I was not open to other people at all before. I'm really grateful.

"Everybody at the [Pulse] center is amazing. I consider them to be very, very good friends. They're open. I can talk to them about anything. I feel like if I have an issue now, if I'm having trouble integrating a lesson or anything in general, I can contact anybody that I've met there. The people who were also at the retreat with me, those are going to be lifelong friends. I definitely made some amazing connections because of it. Tatyana especially, like, I've gotten really close to her. She's an amazing person.

"So, I went back and the second time I went I was a little shocked by the strength of the medicine. I did twelve ceremonies. The first ceremony was very, very overwhelming and I didn't think that I would be able to drink eleven more times. The most shocking difference between my first and second trip was just the strength of the medicine.

"I continued to work on everything that I uncovered during my first session. Wiler [shaman at Pulse Tours and Ayahuasca Adventure Center] actually asked me to come back because even during my fourth ceremony, I uncovered a lot of things. He said he could help me with that. I basically picked up where I left off, so I would set my intention for what I discovered in the last ceremony. We would address that exact thing in the ceremony, whatever my intention was, that's what was addressed. Then something else would come up, so we'd work on that in the next one.

"When I came back, I noticed that my work was just...I was able to focus on it better and it's just gotten a lot cleaner. I feel like I have more ideas for designs. I don't really know if that's where they're coming from, but I definitely feel more inspired.

"It was also difficult to come back because before I wasn't allowing myself to feel anything or process anything. Then you're so different and you come back into a world that's exactly the same. Everybody else is the same, nothing has changed, but you still have to try to work those lessons in there.

"When I came home, I was feeling everything. It was really overwhelming because I'd never allowed myself to do that. I learned to just be emotional and acknowledge that I have emotions, and if I do experience anger, which I don't very often anymore, I'm able to look at it and see where it's coming from and address it from a place of being centered instead of just lashing out in rage like I used to. I would just be angry and not understand why or try to stop it or anything like that.

"I'm just emotionally a lot more stable for sure. That's been the biggest difference for me. That was one of the main issues I went to Peru with. I wasn't able to cry. I never allowed myself to cry, and certainly not in front of other people. Then, after my fourth ceremony, I was able to talk about sexual trauma that I had just learned about in front of twenty-five strangers—not really strangers, but people I wouldn't talk about that kind of stuff in front of. I cried. I was just like, 'Oh my God, I'm crying in front of these people and they don't even care.'

"The ceremonies can be hard. I had a ceremony where I was shown every horrible thing, every time I've hurt somebody throughout my whole life. There are a lot of things to see because I spent my whole life being angry and taking it out on people I love. I experienced all the pain I caused from their perspective. It was horrifying. It was a really rough night. I felt really ashamed and just like I was a monster. It was not a good night, but I forgave myself.

"Now I'm so much more aware of the way that I treat other people. I have a lot more empathy toward them. When I see people acting the way that I used to, instead of being like, 'Oh, they're a jerk,' I'm like, 'Oh, they're suffering and they need love.' I definitely look at people in a totally different way now.

"Professionally, the response I've gotten to my designs since I returned has been just overwhelming. It's crazy to me, having never been artistic before, to have people pay as much as they do for something that I created. I'm still really just kind of in shock that it's happening at all. The way that I've been designing pieces has been primarily custom orders. People will contact me, and I'll show them all the stones that I have or find the stones that they need and then build a design around it. I work with only sterling and fine silver. I hand fabricate.

"This is truly a labor of love for me. I'm still blown away that I get to sit here all day and play with beautiful gemstones and silver and fire. It's so much fun. I'm very, very lucky."

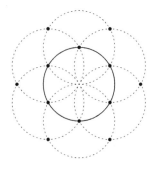

CHAPTER TWO

WHATEVER IT TAKES

A LOT OF PEOPLE WHO HEAR ABOUT MY TRAVEL adventures think, *I want to do that, too,* but they don't know where to start, what to plan, or how to proceed. Even though I have largely learned by trial and error, I do recommend certain strategies to anyone considering adventurous travel.

FINDING FUNDS

A big obstacle most travelers face is financing the trip. You might be surprised, though, by the number of ways you can engineer travel so it doesn't cost a lot of money out of your pocket. With access to search engines these days, it's really easy. The array of choices is always changing and new opportunities pop up all the time.

TEACH ENGLISH

One common way to secure some time in another country is to teach English, though not everyone is a shoo-in for this type of post.

In many places, you need a bachelor's degree to teach English, but in some places—South America, for example—you can usually get away with not having a degree. Franchises like Berlitz have prerequisites to weed out people who are only interested in travel or who aren't educated enough to teach English.

My personal experience with higher education has been mixed, but I do recommend that young people pursue a bachelor's degree. A four-year degree is the new high school diploma. Getting that piece of paper is often crucial to getting your foot in the door. Having a specialization that goes on top of your undergraduate degree can be valuable as well. Master's degrees and doctorates can put you a cut above the rest.

The qualifications don't end there. In about 90 percent of the chain schools, you will also need some kind of certificate, like Teacher of English as a Foreign Language (TOEFL) or Teacher of English as a Second Language (TESL).

Once you have cleared the education hurdles, companies will ask about your practical experience. Agencies will want to know about any work—paid or volunteer—you've done in other countries.

Proving your credentials in some countries in Asia, the Middle East, and Europe can be even more complex. In some European countries, for example, you need to have a notarized copy of your degree. The reward for this hassle is that you can spend six months or a year in one country or region and earn money while you do it. In Asia and the Middle East, you can actually teach for a couple of years, save some money, pay off student loans, or just save enough money to travel even more.

In Asia, many jobs offer attractive vacation packages as part of the language-teaching deal. You can explore the region, see the culture, and even learn some additional languages at the same time.

GET YOUR HANDS DIRTY

One fairly recent addition to low-budget travel options with a cultural bent is WWOOFING. That stands for World Wide Opportunity on Organic Farms or Willing Workers on Organic Farms. Farms around the world welcome workers who help out on the farm for free or for a small stipend and get to spend time in the rural areas of a country. People with trades experience are good candidates for WWOOFING, but it's also an option for anyone willing to get his or her hands dirty for a few hours a day in exchange for immersion in another culture. Anyone with horticultural, carpentry, electrical, or plumbing experience would be a natural candidate.

About sixty countries around the world have working holiday visa programs that provide a short-term working visa. It was a holiday visa that allowed me to stay and work in Australia. This arrangement is different from a long-term professional visa, where you're expected to immigrate into the country. The short-term version is meant to be temporary but allows you to get a job in order to pay your travel expenses. Just be sure to do your research because job availability in any given field can vary widely from place to place and tends to fluctuate over time.

Realize, too, that temporary gigs like this add value to your résumé in the future, not necessarily because of the nature of the work, but because international work experience demonstrates to future employers that you are an independent problem solver. Any sort of travel is applicable, but honestly, if you just say you went to Thailand for six months, all that tells a prospective employer is that you were jumping off cliffs into beautiful blue water, maybe drinking buckets of vodka Red Bulls, and going to full-moon parties. If, on the other hand, you've been in Thailand teaching English, volunteering at a wildlife preserve, or working at an orphanage, that shows you held down some responsibility while you were there, learned a lot more about the culture than your counterparts who were not working, and probably learned some of the language, too.

SEMESTER ABROAD

Field study abroad with a university program offers a reliable, predictable way to live and learn in a new country. My trip to Australia started with a college field study. We went to do a population density study on a species of crab on Vanuatu. It was just a three-week trip, but it gave me some leverage later when applying for a fisheries observer job because I had been studying species and taking detailed observations while in Australia.

I absolutely recommend that students take the opportunity to go abroad with their university programs. Not only do you get an international adventure and intercultural immersion experience, but you are also working toward your degree at the same time.

HOSTEL HOPPING

Thousands of hostels around the world offer not only cheap places to stay and a community of fellow travelers, but many have work options as well. If you go to a country and fall in love with it, you can always work or volunteer in a backpacker hostel. Pay is meager, but you will meet and get to know people from all around the world. Plus, you can usually get free room and board.

TRAVEL SCHOLARSHIPS

I've recently become aware of something called travel scholarships. A number of volunteer organizations and travel blogger sites such as World Nomads or Volunteer-forever.com sponsor travelers who will then write about their adventures. To get the gig, you submit writing samples, maybe a résumé or school transcript, to enter the competition for trips. Once selected, the company pays for your flight to some exotic destination with the understanding that you will write about it for them. A friend of mine has applied to World Nomads to go on a travel scholarship to New Zealand on a mountain excursion.

CROWDFUNDING

With the right networks and some social media savvy, crowdfunding can provide money for travel as well. Platforms like GoFundMe have worked well for some Pulse Tour participants. Not too long ago, a man from England made a video and ran a GoFundMe campaign asking the world to send him to Peru for some healing with ayahuasca. He got it. Volunteerforever.com has its own fund-raising platform; a quick Google search will reveal many others.

BUILD A MUSE

If you want to get creative, there are lots of different ways to design travel plans that won't break the bank. One method that resonates with me is what Tim Ferriss, in his book *The 4-Hour Workweek*, calls building a muse. Essentially, a muse is a low-input business, perhaps online, that funds your particular lifestyle.

Ferriss suggests that you calculate your target monthly income by making a plan that details what you want to do and exactly how much it is going to cost. Next, identify market niches available to you to create an online shop to generate that income.

This approach can take time to build up but can continue to make money long into the future.

WORK REMOTELY

More and more, people are able to work remotely from anywhere in the world, whether for a company they already work with or on a freelance basis. Using technologies like GoToMeeting, WebEX, and Skype, you can earn as you go...anywhere!

Pulse takes advantage of this option. Although our center is physically grounded in Peru, we don't actually have an office. Our management team is me, Tatyana Telegina, Melissa Stangl, and the folks on the ground at the center, but we are rarely all in the same location. We have run the business this way from the beginning, and it gives us all incredible freedom.

Remote work is a fantastic way to do business. It may require a little creativity to convince an employer that you can get the same amount of work done at the same quality while working from a remote location, but it's the truth. Most people are filling up the hours in the office just to meet their forty-hour-a-week minimum; in reality, they could probably do their job in about 60 percent of that time. Working remotely, you have fewer distractions and wasteful meetings, freeing you up to more efficiently accomplish your actual work.

CURRENCY CONVERSION

Another tip from Tim Ferriss is to leverage currency conversions in different countries. If you're in the United States, making enough money to save a few thousand dollars, you can take that cash to a number of countries that have much lighter lifestyle expenses. If you're creative about what you spend your money on, drink the local beers, and travel like a local, you can really stretch out a dollar. For example, US to Brazilian currency conversion is currently in our favor, at about double what it was when I was there in 2011.

VOLUNTEERISM

Money, of course, isn't everything. Plenty of organizations offer opportunities to travel and volunteer. Volunteerforever.com is one example. Keep in mind that these opportunities are often not entirely cost-free. You may be spending money to go work somewhere, but you can get a lot of personal satisfaction out of it, as well as a valuable entry on your résumé.

What you're paying for in a volunteer trip is an intercultural experience and a chance to help local communities around the world. Agencies like Planeterra (a nonprofit run by G Adventures) have operations set up in a wide range of communities.

WHO GOES THERE?

People who embark on these adventures come from all walks of life. Anyone from age eighteen to sixty-five, or even older, can gain a lot from travel. Under eighteen is tricky, because many organizations are concerned about taking on the responsibility of an underage participant, but there are school programs for that age group. Similarly, some excursions are geared for seniors. There really is something for everyone.

STAYING THE COURSE

Planning a trip is exciting, but executing it can often be a challenge, especially on a psychological level. There's a fairly predictable "culture shock curve" that travelers experience, and it can be helpful to know this before you begin.

Cultural adaptation runs a course that looks a bit like a sine wave. You start off in high spirits. You're going on vacation! This honeymoon phase lasts a month or two, and then the curve starts sloping downward. Soon enough, it dips below the median line and you start feeling hostility. You've had enough of this culture! All you want to do is go home to familiarity.

It can be helpful to realize that it's fine to pull back a bit at this point and regroup. Hole up in your hotel room with a Netflix series or whatever feels comforting to you, and then reenter the foreign culture refreshed.

The discomfort of integrating a new culture, however, means you are expanding your boundaries. You are learning something new, and that's what it's all about. When you start to feel a little bit nervous, you know you are entering a period of growth.

After a few months, your cultural adaptation curve will begin to head north again. You may start to find your foibles in this new environment humorous, even enjoyable. About six months in, you will start feeling at home in the new culture.

One interesting thing about the cultural adaptation process is that it happens in reverse when you return home. At first, everyone is happy to see you, and all the familiar sights and sounds make you feel grateful to be home. Soon enough, though, people get used to having you back, routines return, and you remember all the things you didn't like about your home culture. Reintegration takes about six months to feel complete.

The more travel you do, of course, the easier the integration and reintegration processes become. I've moved around so much that the culture shock curve has really tightened up for me. In a matter of weeks, I generally adapt to a new culture with no problem.

LEARN THE LANGUAGE

Cultural integration goes much faster when you learn the language of the locals. Spanish is a great choice, because it's the second or third most spoken language in the world. Spanish is relevant not just in Spain, but in the United States, all through Latin America, Canada, and the Philippines, where Spanish was once the official language.

While language classes are often mandatory in elementary and high school, a lot of students think of the classroom instruction as a joke. I spent five years learning French in school, but I couldn't speak it for the life of me. It was only when I was chasing a French-speaking Swiss girl that I actually studied the language. Unfortunately, French isn't useful in as many places as Spanish.

The other really useful language is Mandarin, which requires learning a whole new system of characters and culture. I found it incredibly difficult. To learn Mandarin, it's helpful to study Chinese culture because there are a lot of cultural nuances in the language that are crucial to successful communication.

I suggest incorporating some language training in your college or university program. If you have a fascination with the south, learn Spanish and Portuguese. If you can't wait to go to Europe, study Spanish and French. For Asia, look at Japanese or Chinese language courses.

In addition to helping you integrate into foreign cultures, language learning sets you up for a rich future. You make yourself that much more attractive to potential employers, even if you don't have the specific skills a particular job calls for. The employer can see from the language and travel experience on your résumé that you are a person who can learn anything.

DOWN UNDER…WAY DOWN

Of course, I didn't start out an expert traveler. I've hit enough walls along the way, both psychologically and physically. We touched on this in the introduction. A closer look will reveal how my rock bottom materialized, and how I began to work my way out of the quagmire I had made of my life.

In May 2009, I went to Australia. My intention was to continue the university-level studies I had begun at Okanagan College in Canada in 2008. After witnessing the destructive force of the tar sands projects in Canada and many social and environmental problems in South America, I had a new mission. I wanted to do something positive for the world and environment. When the opportunity arose to take part in a field study arranged by one of my professors—a conservation project in Vanuatu—I knew I had to go.

My environmental and academic ambitions, as it happened, meshed quite nicely with my personal goals. I was a young man seeking romance, and I had a vision in the back of my mind of falling in love with a beautiful woman in Australia. It may sound hokey, but I had held this vision for years, ever since a psychic told my sister Emily that I was going to go to Australia and meet an incredible, beautiful woman and fall in love. With that in mind, I was ready to stay longer than the three weeks of the university field study; I applied for a working holiday visa, which would allow me to extend my stay for up to six months if I worked for an Australian company.

Always eager for the next adventure, I not only spent time with my student group in Brisbane but also applied to a university in Australia and got accepted. Such easy success seemed like a sure sign that I should stay. I could see myself studying in Australia, loving the tropical climate, and meeting the perfect girl, but the funding I was getting from the Canadian government didn't pay the bills. It amounted to only about $300 a week on top of the international tuition. Going to school in Australia would cost $18,000 a year just for tuition, plus living expenses.

I had been getting some financial support from my family. With that, I may have made my dream scenario in Australia come true, if it weren't for the pesky little economic meltdown of 2008–2009. My parents were quite stressed because they lost about 25 percent of their retirement investments. My father said, "If you want to stay in Australia, that's fine, but you're going to have to do it on your own dime."

OK, I thought, *I'm on my own.* I wasn't worried, though.

I naïvely assumed that I'd just be able to find work, save up lots of money, and be able to pay my tuition and living expenses. Everything would be awesome. Of course, that's not quite what happened.

SELLING OUT

I was fairly smitten with Brisbane right away. I wanted to stay. I immediately started studying the newspaper for jobs and applied for a sales and marketing gig on my second day in Brisbane. The $70 I had to my name bought me the secondhand shirt and tie that saw me through the interview. Not only did I get the position, but I also started the next day with an extremely attractive trainer named Gemma. I was infatuated with her and glad to have her tutor me on my new job: door-to-door, commission-only sales.

We sold automotive servicing packages, little 8-½ × 11-inch cards with service discount coupons on them. It wasn't glamorous work, but I made four sales on the first day. Here I was, with a fresh $250 in my pocket, working with a superhot girl in an amazing part of the world. I thought it might actually work. If I could pull in $1,000 or $1,200 a week, I'd be in good shape.

When my school group was headed back to Canada, I had no trouble deciding to stay behind in Australia. I didn't have enough money to pay to change my flight, so I forfeited my flight home, which seemed like a fine bargain. The honeymoon period didn't last long, though; after a few weeks, it became apparent that Gemma was not interested in me, and the initial bonuses I was getting at work started to run out. I met some good friends, but it became increasingly difficult to bring in enough money to save anything after paying rent, bills, and lifestyle expenses, even though I lived fairly frugally, renting a room in a three-bedroom house.

After two or three months, I started to despise walking around neighborhoods knocking on doors. Some days were both grueling and dispiriting; I'd spend ten hours walking around in the hot sun, knocking on doors, and getting told to get lost, all the while watching for dogs around the corner. Dogs were a real problem; a couple of times I had to run from vicious dogs and jump over fences to get away.

Honestly, my dream job turned out to be the worst sales job I ever had. I was humiliated by having to interrupt people while they were eating dinner to try to sell them this piece of crap. I didn't like getting pushy with people. I would put on a smile and talk to people, but it wasn't like we were having real conversations. Instead of building a relationship, I was only interested in their money. I loathed the work but felt I had to do it to pay my rent. Meantime, fall was approaching, along with new tuition payments. I didn't have the resources to make it work.

With my school start date deferred to January, I was

very discouraged. I wasn't getting any closer to my dream of continuing my studies, and I was looking for yet another job. I started to regret my decision to stay in Australia and wished I had gone back to Canada with my cohort. Government funding would have allowed me to continue my studies, and I probably would have still received some support from my parents. With a little extra part-time work, I could have made it through to my bachelor's degree.

Getting a degree was an important goal. I was twenty-eight years old and had tried many college programs without finishing any to my satisfaction. I felt naked without college credentials. As I grew to dislike sales work more and more, I wasn't able to switch into a new profession without a college degree.

I didn't know what to do next. I was an environmentalist who wanted to do something to help the world, and yet I spent my days doing meaningless sales work. I recognized that the more you do something, the more likely it is you are going to continue to do it—you are getting better at it and solidifying a pattern of behavior—and I didn't want to get stuck in that trap. I was desperate to stop the cycle.

That summer in Australia, I frantically applied to all kinds of jobs, but the Australian economy was fairly protectionist after the financial crisis. Most companies were strict about hiring only Australia or New Zealand residents. At the same time, my visa was running out. The working holiday visa allowed me to work for the whole year but only for six months at any one company. The higher-level, more professional sales jobs I applied for never panned out because the companies were reluctant to hire and train someone who was leaving after only six months.

NOWHERE TO GO BUT UP

I was absolutely stuck. I was just trying, trying, trying, and trying but getting nowhere. Depression hit me hard at this point. I remember one day riding around Byron Bay with some friends, who were all laughing, joking around, and enjoying the beautiful scenery—except me. I was just sitting there in the car, locked in my own head, worrying about everything. I thought, *What the fuck? I'm down here in this incredible place and I'm miserable.* My thoughts actually turned suicidal. I realized that it was a good thing my mother loved me so much because if it wasn't for her, I might just disappear.

The frustrations kept on mounting that fall. I continued to get turned down for work. Desperate for solutions, I finagled a way to get a de facto visa that would let me work in Australia permanently. The de facto visa requires a long-term relationship with an Australian citizen, which I did not have, but there was no way to get past the recruiters without that document. So I got creative and manufactured a visa that would get me in the door that led to a new, salaried job to start in November.

Finally, some of the pressure was off. I looked forward

to the comforts of a company car, cell phone, and computer, along with a promising commission structure. I still didn't have any actual money, though, so once again, my university start date slid into the next term start.

I was still deeply unsettled, so maybe it is not surprising what happened next, although I certainly did not plan it. One night not long after I started working at the new company, I went out to the nightclubs with a friend, had my fair share of whiskey and bourbon but made it home by midnight. I was still restless, so I went for a walk down to South Bank Park and Kangaroo Point, a ridge that extends out into the Brisbane River. The Point features a twenty-meter, sheer cliff that Brisbane residents climb all the time. I had seen people scramble up this rock with harnesses, ropes, helmets, and spotters. But that night—it was November 27, 2009—I was down there by myself with no equipment. The cliff looked totally harmless, wreathed in pink and purple Christmas lights. It looked like a giant pink marshmallow. How dangerous could that be?

I ambled over, touched the rock with my hands, looked up, and just started climbing. I don't think I ever really intended to go all the way up, but it was fun, so I just kept climbing. Once I got past the halfway mark, I thought, *I can probably go all the way up.* I almost got there. I stalled maybe two meters from the top. I could see the wispy grass above me, but there was an overhang between me and solid ground. I couldn't find any grips to grab onto.

I was stuck.

My first instinct was to go back down, but I couldn't get a hold on anything with the slippery dress shoes I was wearing. When down didn't work, I went back up to where I had gotten stuck but couldn't achieve the stability I'd had just moments before. (I was too freaked out at the time to notice how my physical predicament mirrored my life's trajectory to date.)

Panic set in. Shaking, tired, and scared, I looked around and saw an outcropping I might be able to reach if I jumped over to it. So I jumped—and missed, falling straight to the ground about fifteen meters down.

The impact was crushing. My left leg exploded at the femur, which was busted in three different places and sticking out of the side of my leg. The breaks tore the skin across half of my thigh and pulled it up. It was gruesome. My leg, however, may have been the least of my problems, as my pelvis absorbed much of the impact, splitting clean in half right in the middle—a vertical shear fracture—and jutting upward into my abdomen.

I can still feel the impact to this day, although at the time, I was in a state of shock. I didn't have a lot of feeling in my leg and pelvis, but I knew something was really wrong because I couldn't move. From my landing place in the gravel, I could see some teenagers chilling out down in the park, so I started screaming for help. My voice was muffled because the chunk of bone in my abdomen made it hard to get enough air. The kids ultimately heard me, though, and came over. The first thing one guy said was, "Holy shit, dude, look at your leg!" I just begged them to call an ambulance. In minutes, I was on my way to a nearby hospital with a needle in my neck sending me gratefully off to la-la land.

Whatever they gave me made the next few hours bearable, even enjoyable. I was so high I laughed hysterically while they cut off my jeans and pulled my leg back into place. It looked like a wet noodle. I couldn't stop laughing.

I spent the next few days getting stitched up and outfitted with a strange exoskeleton apparatus the doctors used to hold my bones in place, getting some relief from a morphine drip, and waiting for surgeries. Soon, I was the not-so-proud owner of a titanium rod that spanned from knee to hip and a titanium plate screwed into my realigned pelvis.

If there was any silver lining in the weeks I spent healing in the hospital suffering the indignity of complete incapacitation, bedpans, and all, it was the time I got to spend just hanging out with my mother, who had traveled from Canada to be at my bedside.

Otherwise, I was alone with my thoughts, and my thoughts were grim. The accident brought up some childhood traumas and grief from the past, putting me in a psychologically fragile frame of mind. Plus, I had racked up $40,000 in medical bills, I didn't have insurance, and I didn't have any money. Meanwhile, I was hooked on pain-killers in the hospital; I always took the maximum dose every time and had to ask for new prescriptions sooner than I should have. And I was looking at four months on crutches. My circumstances had gone swiftly from bad to much, much worse; it was as though the universe was just telling me, "Leave Australia. You are not meant to be here. Go."

A SEED IS PLANTED

As I was lying there all busted up and thinking about what a disaster the past year had been, I remembered what I had read years earlier about ayahuasca. I knew it was something I was eventually going to do because there was so much psychological garbage going through my mind that needed clearing out. In the hospital, I got really serious about doing it. Honestly, it scared the hell out of me. All of the things I heard about ayahuasca indicated it was an insanely potent, powerful psychedelic. When you took it, you confronted all your demons, your past traumas, and any hidden parts of your psyche. All of this was supposed to come up during the ayahuasca ceremonies, and those were exactly the things I knew I needed to face. Ayahuasca represented a way forward for me, a way out of the mental misery I was enduring on a daily basis.

I didn't talk to many people about my interest in aya-huasca at the time. It was only a few years ago, but most people considered plant medicine a fringe, subculture scene. I did write in a journal, though, to help me deal with everything that was coming up, and some of the writing was very intense, though enlightening. I visualized the garbage I was carrying around as little orbs, each one of them containing some type of self-defeating program, residual trauma, or blockage that led to all of the stupid things I had done in my life. These orbs of negativity floated around me; I was carrying them everywhere I went. From all of the research I had done about ayahuasca, I felt like it offered a way out of this turmoil.

Thank goodness for the manager of the solar company I was working for at the time. He was a motocross racer, so he knew about serious injuries and empathized with my situation. Incredibly, he kept me on staff while I was in the hospital, working with customers I had gone to see before the accident. I actually sold about $50,000 worth of equipment during my stay in the hospital. He thought I was a superstar for that, so I continued to work with him after I got out, selling subsidized solar panel installations that would allow Australian homeowners to sell solar power from their homes back into the grid.

It was good work, but I wasn't feeling great. I continued popping OxyContin like it was going out of style and partying with friends I'd met at the door-to-door sales job. It became clear that the long-postponed April start date at university wasn't going to happen. I didn't want to stay anyway; I felt isolated living so far from my family. Then, in March 2010, I got a letter from my dad saying that my childhood dog was on her last legs.

We'd brought Molly into the family when I was in sixth grade, after I had researched breeds and made my case to my parents for either a border collie or an Australian shepherd. I begged them for years before I found an ad for an Australian shepherd-border collie-cross puppy for $30. I spent so many days training her and hiking with her in the forest behind our house. Dad's letter brought the sad news that at seventeen, Molly's hiking and playing days were over.

DETOURS

That letter gave me the last bit of evidence I needed that it was time to pack up my Australian life and head back to Canada. On my way home, I decided to stop in Peru to visit an ayahuasca center I had been researching since my days in the hospital. I had started paying attention to the ayahuasca community and heard a lot about this place, so I flew to Lima from Los Angeles instead of heading directly home.

I had never been to Peru, although I had traveled in almost every other country in South America, and I didn't enter the country with much of a plan. I knew the ayahuasca center was holding a retreat on a certain date, but I didn't contact them because I knew I couldn't really afford it. I was hoping I could just walk up to the gates and the spiritually enlightened group would naturally want to help and heal me, so they would let me in.

Surely, I looked like a sorry case, because I had run out of OxyContin—right before I left Australia, the doctors refused to prescribe any more—so I was going through the most hellish withdrawal imaginable. It was like nothing I had ever experienced before, not at all like a hangover where you just feel a little off for a day or two. No, this started twelve hours after I took my last pill in the middle of the day. By that night, the cramps in my back were so bad I couldn't sleep.

The doctors had told me to wean myself off the pills, but I didn't listen. I couldn't control my consumption, so I opted to go cold turkey instead. That was a huge mistake; I just lay there in agony. The muscle spasms and creepy-crawly twitchy feeling were unbearable. I couldn't drive or anything. It was simply too much to take, so I went rummaging in my pill bag, turned up some ibuprofen and some acetaminophen with codeine in it, which was helpful. I got more codeine, so that eased the agony as I headed to Peru, though I wasn't in the best shape to deal with the 3,400-meter elevation in Cusco.

Not surprisingly, I got altitude sickness right away. I didn't suffer from edema, but the fatigue was really severe. I camped out in my hotel room for days. If I had to get up and go anywhere, I was out of breath and almost passing out. The steep landscape made it very hard to get around. A few days of rest helped me acclimatize to the altitude, so I decided to get up and try to socialize. This impulse led me straight to Loki Hostel, which had a reputation as a party hostel. Once there, I met a crew of Australians celebrating Australia-New Zealand Army Corps day, or Anzac Day, a major holiday in Australia and New Zealand. The main activity on this holiday was drinking, and drinking was something I was very good at. Plus, I had just come from Australia, so I felt a bit of a fraternal connection with these guys.

After a full day of drinking games, things got even crazier. We headed out to a *discoteca* in the main square and partied with a whole bunch of people, dancing it up, having a good time. Around three o'clock in the morning, I left to go back to my hotel, which was very different from the idea most of us have of hotels. It was a small, traditional guest house, on a dark, cobblestone back street, surrounded by huge stone buildings and walls. Cusco has maintained and restored a lot of its ancient stonework, so I was looking at stones that were fitted together almost seamlessly and had stood for thousands of years.

The front of my hotel was one of these tall stone walls, with no windows at all, only a looming set of iron-hinged hardwood doors. I had to knock on the doors and hope someone would come out and open them. I stood there smoking a cigarette in the street at three o'clock in the morning, when out of the darkness, a car pulled up beside me. A guy jumped out of the passenger seat and the next thing I knew, he was in my face with a machete. In a quick blur of activity, two more men got out of the back seats and cleaned out my pockets. They took my wallet, my phone, and my money. Everything was gone. They even stole my ChapStick! Within maybe forty-five seconds they jumped back in the car and drove off. The robbery was lightning fast; I didn't know what had hit me.

I finally made it into the hotel, where I attempted to sleep off the shock and the drinks. In the morning, I struggled to come to grips with what had happened the night before. Surely I couldn't be penniless? I checked the depths of my pockets and came up with one bill for ten Peruvian *soles*, which was about three US dollars. It was enough to buy me some soup from a local market for breakfast. It was delicious.

Pleasure soon turned to pain, though, when I started to feel nauseous a couple of hours later. I came down with the most violent case of food poisoning I have ever heard of. I spent two day holed up in my hotel room, violently purging from both ends, barely making it from bed to bathroom and back. I could see I was simply on the wrong path. I was getting handed smackdown after smackdown.

All I wanted was to go home to Mommy, to a place where I could recover. That meant making the detestable call back to Canada asking my dad for enough money to fly home. I got the regular speech, of course, about how much he hated paying for us kids to travel the world and how we should just settle down and get jobs. But in the end, he said, "OK, fine, I'll buy your flight home, but this is the last time."

THE WINDING PATH HOME

I was relieved, but my adventures on this journey were not quite over yet. On my way from Lima to Cusco at the beginning of the trip, I had made a friend who encouraged me that I was on the right path with my interest in ayahuasca. I had been standing in front of the bus station having a smoke with everyone else and caught sight of this guy who intrigued me. He looked like he was from British Columbia—he sported a sandy blond mop of hippie hair, a wild beard, and rugged clothing—so I approached him.

I complimented his Native American tattoos and asked if he was from BC. He was, indeed, and we chatted together for the entire bus ride. I discovered he had been in Peru doing an ayahuasca retreat in the jungle. He said it was incredible. He had nothing but good—albeit challenging—experiences with the medicine, and also mentioned that he was involved with the Native American Church in New Mexico.

He had come to New Mexico from British Columbia on a golf scholarship, of all things. He started out super-preppy, sports-minded, and generally very straightedge but ended up disillusioned and angry about the area's history and the way Native Americans were treated by the Europeans. He wound up dropping out of university to join the Native American Church. His native name was Bahu, and that's how I knew him.

Bahu got deeply involved in the plant medicine community in New Mexico, participating in ritualistic religious ceremonies that used peyote as a sacrament. He had even smuggled some peyote in a jar down from the States into Peru. When we met, he invited me to go and take some peyote with him at some point during our stay in Cusco, but we parted ways upon arrival, and I lost several days to the altitude sickness, mugging, and food poisoning described earlier.

I didn't talk with Bahu again for five days or more, but after I changed my flight, he called me up at the hotel and we traded stories. His week had been at least as spectacular as mine. Hiking in the hills overlooking the city, he found a place to meditate high in the mountains. It was the perfect spot for meditation, until he fell into a trance and tumbled off the rocks. He emerged from the hospital a few days later all busted up, with bruises and cuts all over his face, arms, and shoulders. We were quite a rough-looking pair after a week in Cusco.

Meeting Bahu was really a turning point for me, though I didn't know it at the time. He invited me to meet him the next day to do a peyote ceremony up in the mountains. He brought all of his tools—feathers, crystals, and Native artifacts—and initiated the ceremony by chanting some Native American songs that he learned in New Mexico, creating his sacred space. The peyote was in powdered form, mixed with water to turn it into a paste. It tasted horrible.

I didn't have a lot of the peyote because I was a little bit apprehensive about trying it for the first time. The effect was mild, and we spent the day exploring Inca ruins up in the hills, visiting the Temple of the Moon and some other places. We rented horses and rode around all day. It was beautiful, but I learned another lesson that day: the sun is really powerful at that elevation. On top of all the other damage my body had recently suffered, I added the worst sunburn of my life.

Sun scorched but elated to have met Bahu, one of my first true teachers, I was ready to head back to Canada for a while, knowing in the back of my mind that I had an open invitation from Bahu to come to New Mexico to do an ayahuasca ceremony with his group.

WORKING IT OUT

Once back in Canada, I needed to get work and earn some money. As it happened, my father, my uncle, and two of my cousins had started up a solar panel company in response to Ontario's newly minted feed-in tariff program, which dovetailed perfectly with what I was doing in Australia.

I worked for them for a few months in a sales role, but ultimately I was determined to move into the environmental sector. That summer, I located a job as a fisheries observer for marine research in British Columbia. The job involved riding commercial fishing boats—bottom draggers, trawlers—for a few days or weeks at a time. It sounded like joining the cast of television's *Deadliest Catch*. The fishermen would bring up a net full of ten thousand pounds of fish and dump it on the deck, where I would document the species of fish they were catching, what they kept, and what they tossed overboard. The goal was to monitor the people who were extracting natural resources in order to minimize environmental damage and preserve species.

I convinced them I was suitable for the job because I had the required one year of postsecondary education, which I earned at Okanagan College in 2008 to 2009, and experience traveling the world with my backpack. They knew I was suited to the adventurous, rugged, and nomadic aspects of the work. They also knew I had experience working with diverse groups of people, which was perfect because this was a particularly sensitive position. The fishermen didn't particularly want to have someone on their boat watching them and writing down everything they were doing. I never felt like an outsider, though, perhaps because of the close quarters.

Picture me on a tin can, floating in the middle of a

vast amount of water and space, yet unable to walk any farther than the boundaries of the tin can for two weeks. The machinery on the boat was constantly running; huge cranes pulled up the nets while the boat got slammed around by waves. The fishermen were true professionals, and really, really tough guys. Their job was dangerous, the weather was temperamental, and it was wild to be out there in a storm.

A big storm hit us on my second or third trip. I was hired to go aboard the *Viking Moon*, a sixty-foot aluminum boat. It was really light and high in the water before it got filled with fish. We were going out to fish thornyheads, which are a delicacy on the Japanese market. The place to go for thornyheads was way up to the top of the Queen Charlotte Islands, and this boat was really slow.

All the fishermen were complaining about how the guy who owned the boat was a terrible penny pincher; he came from a wealthy fisher family but had squandered away a lot of their money. Running these boats is expensive. You're burning diesel fuel, paying for food, and of course paying the fisheries observer's salary. We had gone a long way on this trip, but the nets weren't coming up with much. Morale was pretty low, and here I was on a boat with a dozen angry fishermen, rough-and-tumble guys fresh from the oil fields or logging operations, many of them hard drinkers and tough talkers. It got pretty tense even before the hurricane winds hit.

The storm caught up with us in the middle of the Queen Charlotte Strait; hundred-kilometer-an-hour winds and massive waves assaulted our boat. We were running light, just bobbing up and down in this big boat, getting smashed by waves, and rolling left and right.

At one point, I was up in the cabin with the captain looking around at everything wide-eyed, half superexcited and half scared to death. Seeing these thirty-foot or even fifty-foot waves rise in front of you is pretty incredible. It's tough to even stand up.

That night, I was down in my stateroom with the door latched open so I could see out into the galley. From my bunk, I was watching one of the fishermen sitting at a table when we got broadsided by a huge wave. My side of the boat went down, so I just rolled up against the wall in my bunk. Meanwhile, this other guy was thrust off his seat and flew in midair from one side of the room to the other. The boat was hanging at a ninety-degree angle.

It could have ended badly, but the boat ended up righting itself. The trip continued through several more storms. We were docked up a lot. Finally, as early winter set in after forty-four days, the trip was called off.

Before it was all over, we did have one tow that made up for a lot. When the guys pulled up the net, they knew they had a heavy catch. It looked to be about seven thousand pounds of fish, and everyone was thrilled. Then they dropped the net.

Inside was a three-thousand-pound basking shark. Incredibly, it seemed to still be alive. I tried to save it. Its gills were just packed with fish, so I figured it was having trouble getting oxygen. I washed it off with a hose, pumping saltwater through its gills trying to revive it, but it didn't survive. We had to use the crane to lift it over the side of the boat, which was pretty amazing, yet sad, to watch.

In August 2010, when I first went out to Victoria, British Columbia, to do the three-week training program for this job, I got a call from Bahu, who was hosting three ayahuasca ceremonies at a private ranch in a remote corner of New Mexico. I mentioned something to my employers about a wedding I had to attend and took a few days off my training to make the trip down.

At this juncture, I was an ayahuasca virgin because I didn't actually make it to the retreat center in Peru. I was scared going into the ceremonies, but I knew it was something I needed to do. I was ready to engage with the medicine and see what it had for me. I didn't know it then, but I was about to learn many of the things that would lead to the business I eventually started and the life I now lead. One of the things I have learned from ayahuasca, though, is that everything, even all the regrets I've had and all the mistakes I've made, all led me to where I needed to be. This was just a first step.

DESERT NIGHTS

I arrived in Albuquerque, New Mexico, on a Friday night. It was my first time in any of the southern states, and I loved the gritty, rocky, rugged landscape from the start. Anticipation for my very first ayahuasca ceremony made me jittery but excited. This ceremony would be a rite of passage into a more mature version of myself, and I was eager to begin.

I had a beautiful drive out to a place called Gila, New Mexico, through wide-open space and incredible scenery. There, I was reunited with Bahu, who was busy preparing sage bundles with his girlfriend, doing yoga, and getting ready for the ceremony.

All of the participants, including the shaman, were Americans. The shaman described the upcoming experience as boarding an airplane together, traveling around up in the sky, and coming back down together. He explained the science of the medicine and the origins of the particular batch of medicine he had brought from Peru. It was a concentrated, thick syrup made with ayahuasca and chacruna, the traditional Shipibo composition of the brew. He cautioned that it was very strong and very high quality.

Etiquette was simple. Stay in the ceremonial space, don't talk, don't flash lights around in people's eyes, and try not to make much noise. We sat in a screened-in, second-story room with views of an endless sky filled with the creamy oranges, yellows, and pinks of sunset. The stage was set for a spiritual experience; the surroundings felt energetically charged.

I didn't know what to expect. I may have been a little overconfident, thinking that my experiences with mushrooms and LSD would have prepared me for what was to come. Still, I was nervous about what the universe had in store for me. Just before the ceremony, I went outside to ground myself. I took some sand in my hands and rubbed them together, *Gladiator*-style, and looked up at the sky, saying, "Show me what you've got!"

BOARDING THE PLANE

I had a feeling I was in for something big, but I had no way of knowing how powerful the experience would be. Anyone who has used ayahuasca can attest that it's really impossible to fathom until you encounter it personally.

The shaman offered up doses in shot glasses. He had drawn lines on the glass so you could gauge how much you were taking. I took a full shot glass the first time. Everyone else took their doses and we all went back to our personal spaces.

The retreat providers had set up some pillows and blankets, and we were encouraged to bring a comfort object as well. I had a small travel pillow, crystals, stones, bones, feathers, and the small Shipibo tapestry Bahu had given me in Peru.

As I settled in and got comfortable, I felt the effects

come on. One of the scary aspects of ayahuasca is that it can make you feel nervous at first. It feels like it's coming on really fast and strong, and you don't know how far it's going to go. This was fairly mild and manageable, though. I felt some changes happening in my body and I started to feel high, but I wasn't getting any visual effects. A couple of surges coursed through me, but I wasn't breaking through a portal the way the shaman had described it. I was able to get up, walk around, and go out on the patio and have a cigarette. I noticed others were deep into it, making noises, sobbing, or lying down and meditating with their eyes closed, while I was up wandering around. I wondered if it was working or not.

FLYING HIGH

After two hours, the shaman called for anyone who wanted a second dose. Remembering what he had said about taking enough to cross over the portal, I drank another half glass and went back to my spot. Very quickly, the medicine took hold, and this time it was unmistakable. It simply surged in me. I felt myself climb that slope up into the infinite space of ayahuasca; it steepened and I ascended even more quickly. I had visions of my sisters and their smiling faces. They kept me grounded. I felt feminine energy all around me, embodied by breaths that were visible in the air.

Ayahuasca offers an overwhelming sensory experience,

and it was magnified by the music that began around this time. Several musicians and the shaman were playing instruments and singing *icaros*—songs specifically used in ayahuasca ceremonies to channel energy or healing. I felt I was losing control as Bahu sang over me, chanting the word *ohm* and playing a long instrument that emitted a similar tone. The sound became color, and that frequency started shooting right through me. The vibrations emanated from him and traveled through my chest. At the same time, the shaman was shaking a leaf rattle—a *chakapa*—over me as well. I was inundated with sensation.

I had initially been worried about vomiting, but after the first dose I was feeling pretty confident that I had the nausea under control. There would be no purging for me tonight, I was sure. When the vibrations traveled through me and the colors swirled around me, though, the urge to vomit came on in a split second. I sat up fast, only to realize I had no motor skills, it was completely dark, and I had no idea where my purge bucket was. I couldn't find the bucket for the life of me, but the first wave of vomit came on anyway. Then another. I was still determined not to let go until I found that bucket, but my sensory perception was so altered and my muscular capabilities so reduced that I just couldn't do it. By the time the third wave hit, I just popped like a champagne bottle.

It went all over the floor, all over me, and it just kept coming. In ceremonial etiquette this is the worst thing that could happen. It's awful for you, but it's also horrifying for those next to you and the facilitators who have to clean it up, quickly, in the dark. A facilitator came over and shone an LED light around to find my bucket, stationed me over that, and got to work cleaning up. I could have stayed over that bucket for another half an hour, but she helped me stand up and escorted me to the washroom to clean up.

I was chagrined not only that I had vomited on the floor but that there was also so much of it. This was my own fault, no doubt, because I had ignored the fasting recommendations and had stopped at a gas station for beer and burritos on my way to the retreat. Now I was stuck in a washroom that only afforded a tiny trickle of water from the faucet, trying to clean myself up while a line grew outside because I was hogging the facilities. All the while, the walls twisted and morphed around me. I looked in the mirror and started laughing hysterically. I thought, *You dipshit. You wanted something intense. Here you go!*

SAFE LANDING

The facilitator helped me back to the ceremonial space, noting that I should avoid the Persian rug if I had to vomit again, but I assured her I was fine. Things took a more contemplative turn after this. I had some really wild visuals and did some grieving for my dog, Molly. I was still processing the trauma of losing such an important part of my upbringing. The ceremony allowed me the space and solitude to grieve about that and shed some tears. I felt I was finally able to say good-bye.

I had a lot of questions that I hoped to answer through this ceremony, and it helped tremendously. I went in wondering if I should take the fisheries job, and I got a clear answer that yes, it was an adventure I should embrace even if it would only be temporary. I also had a lot of regrets and guilt over mistakes I had made, failed relationships, and bad decisions in my past. I had a strong vision during this ceremony that erased all of that for me. It was like I was somebody else looking at me and seeing all the imperfections and injuries, yet feeling such a sense of love and forgiveness for this guy, which flipped a switch for me to move from sabotaging myself with self-destructive behavior to actually doing the things that could help me get ahead.

I could see that it had been so important for me that all of those things had happened along the way because everything, no matter how wrong it seemed at the time, had led me to one beautiful, perfect point in time and space. Everything was a journey leading up to this point. I wasn't making endless mistakes; I was following my own personal path. Knowing that allowed me to resolve lot of guilt and take responsibility for the future.

As the ceremony wound down, we were outside in the mountains, under a clear night sky with the moon and a few stars shining among the wispy clouds, and I looked up and realized I had just opened up a whole new dimension of life. I had a boundless appreciation for the great mysteries of the universe and all that I was yet to learn but felt certain I was bound to learn.

The next day, we met with the shaman and the facilitators to share our experience. I said I felt like I had discovered the meaning of five words I thought I knew but didn't understand until now. Those words were *intensity*, *love*, *medicine*, *agony*, and *profundity*. The experience was so transformative I wrote a highly descriptive e-mail of the event and sent it to everyone in my contacts list. That really launched my path on ayahuasca. I knew I had to bring it to others.

SHIMBRE

My next step was to learn as much as I could about ayahuasca, the ceremonies, and how people could access it. I was following the Shimbre Shamanic Center's website and learning about the founder's life. Rob Velez was a Wall Street banker who suffered serious depression, stress, and anxiety from his high-finance life. He broke through that by working with shaman Jose Pineda Vargas and was so moved by his experience that he started a healing center in the Amazon basin of Peru. Shimbre was hugely successful in 2010, when Rob was talking about it online and recruiting volunteers to come down and serve as chefs, artists, and writers.

I jumped on the resident writer position because it would put me on-site, where I would write about the experience. I sent Rob a couple of writing samples and told him about my own ayahuasca experience. When I got the OK from Rob, I took the month of February 2011 off from my fisheries work to travel back down to Peru. Once there, I started a blog that began with the story of my first ayahuasca experience in the Amazon jungle and segued into recording the workings of the Shimbre center.

A couple of things came out of my time at Shimbre. I gained insight into the operations of such a center, and I also did a lot of very deep personal exploration and intro-spection. Challenges came at me from every direction. Living in the jungle, fasting, learning from the people who worked there, studying the shaman's medicines—it was a lot to take in. I purged in every ceremony, which served to cleanse my physical body and my energetic body as well. My thinking became clearer and my emotional state was more stable.

The medicine has proven scientific effects on mood over the long term, raising the "happy chemicals," sero-tonin and dopamine. Ayahuasca isn't like MDMA or cocaine, where the mood-lifting chemicals surge while you are using the drug but leave you with a deficit of those same chemicals afterward.

In the moment, ayahuasca may actually ask more of you. You do feel a state of bliss and tranquility while you're on the medicine, as long as you're not writhing in discomfort. After the main effects subside, though, you achieve an overall sense of well-being that can last for days or weeks, depending on how well you treat your body after the experience.

A 2004 study by Dennis McKenna looked into ayahuasca's effects on regular users, such as the members of União do Vegetal, a religious group in Brazil. McKenna uncovered several interesting trends, such as lower levels of drug and alcohol abuse, domestic violence, and criminal activity alongside higher levels of serotonin. Regular use of ayahuasca can bring those levels up for the long term.

I felt those beneficial psychological effects in myself in terms of a greater sense of well-being, and a tempering of my ego. I found myself becoming more independent in my thought processes and less dependent on the approval of others. It was a time of mental growth.

The physical effects were remarkable, too. I was able to quit smoking, improve my diet, and dramatically reduce my alcohol consumption.

As my mind cleared, I began brainstorming for the first time what would become Pulse Tours and Ayahuasca Adventure Center. I wasn't interested in replicating Shimbre, where the focus was on the shamans and their traditions. I wanted a place in the jungle, but I wanted it to be a little more lighthearted and fun. This was the first time in my life I had been able to rein in all of my scattered passions and skills and focus them on one ideal outcome. In the past, I had not been able to wholeheartedly look beyond a six-month to one-year time frame. I could never fully define what I wanted to do with my life. My newfound certainty supercharged me with the energy I needed.

Up until this point, I felt like I was a jack of all trades but master of none. I had technical experience, tourism experience, and sales experience, but where was it all leading? As the concept of building a retreat center in the jungle grew in my mind, I realized I could mix these things together with other skills like language learning and teaching. The new center could be an intercultural integration center with educational programs for foreigners to come and learn language and culture.

I was really psyched to start a center, but I was focused on Brazil and probably a little overoptimistic because of how much I had enjoyed living there. My idea was to have both English and Portuguese language learners in the same place, mixing together and interacting. We would host ceremonies from time to time, but it wouldn't be a full-on shamanic center. Participants would be encouraged to go out and do fun things together outside the center as well.

My notebook quickly filled up with blog posts, site drawings, and business plans. I had my eye on Manaus, with a population of almost two million people. Tourism and teaching English were both big there. I felt confident

I could bring ayahuasca into the mix in a meaningful way.

READING UP

Before I could set up shop in Manaus, however, I was due back in Canada. It seemed like a step back, but returning home led me to some interesting discoveries. I started working on the ocean again, in a little town called Port Hardy. Commercial fishermen made money hand over fist there in the seventies through the nineties, when there were no regulations and the fish stocks were more plentiful. By the time I got up there, though, the economy had gone bust. The fishing industry had been dramatically downsized. Fishermen were required to stick to a quota system, plus they had to pay for the observers. So Port Hardy was a little run-down.

It seems like the least likely place for me to pick up cutting-edge entrepreneurial advice, but that's what happened. Sitting in a café and bookstore, awaiting my next trip out, I noticed Tim Ferriss's book, *The 4-Hour Workweek*, on the shelf. It caught my attention right away. The tag line was: "Escape the 9 to 5, live anywhere, and join the new rich." I was hooked.

I took that book on the boat with me; I must have read it ten times. The sheer number of hours I spent sitting in the stateroom while the fishermen were working was usually overwhelming; now I could use it to read, highlight, take notes, and add tabs to half the pages in this book.

Ferriss's words validated thoughts I had entertained for years. I always felt a bit of the maverick for my critical take on how people were supposed to think and behave in Western culture, and here was a guy with the same thoughts, plus a bunch of tools for escaping the system.

I grabbed Scott Belsky's *Making Ideas Happen* from that same bookstore and devoured it as well. These books came into my life at an important time. They inspired me to go beyond brainstorming to investigating online forums and website platforms like Weebly and WordPress where I could actually make my ideas public.

By June, I felt I had learned all I could at the fisheries job. Brazil was calling, loud and clear, and I heeded its call.

Back in Manaus, I started putting into practice everything I had learned from Ferriss and Belsky. My objective was to locate property, develop my business plan, and make it happen. I used Belsky's action method religiously, writing down my daily action steps, assigning each of those to my current projects, and organizing my life essentially into a series of projects. Some things moved to the back burner occasionally, but overall, I was making progress.

Network engagement was next on my list. I started a Manaus blog, which I sent out to all my contacts every Sunday. Here, I illuminated my objectives, made updates, posted travel photos and information, and just generally mused about the project. I didn't have a big audience; most readers knew me personally, but it still helped keep me on point.

Day-to-day life did its best to keep me from swift headway, however. The visa situation alone was enough to make me crazy. When I applied for a visa and got it, I didn't even think to check it. I just assumed it was a five-year visa with six months available each year. As I was crossing the border, though, the immigration attendant asked me how long I was staying. In my mind, I was thinking, *forever*, but I told him, "Oh, I don't know. Two or three months?" He said, "I'm sorry, sir, your visa is good for only thirty days." Thirty days? Sure enough, when I looked at it, I could clearly see it was a thirty-day, single entry visa.

Still, I was there, so I dug into my English teaching job, only to discover it wasn't as lucrative as I thought it would be. I got only about twenty hours a week of work, and some weeks that meant forty hours of bus rides getting from place to place.

Scouting for a retreat site didn't go much better. I found some half-decent properties in the area, but most were more expensive than I had expected. My very optimistic hope was to get investments from friends and family to fund a time-share scenario, with rooms or bungalows we could rent out. Unfortunately, my timing was off, as jungle tourism in Manaus was declining. G Adventures had even stopped running the trip I had once led.

Brazil did not turn out to be the right place for a center, but I was able to take away many valuable lessons. Business lessons, to be sure, but I also had time to absorb more teachings on ayahuasca and refine my vision of what my ayahuasca center might or might not include.

SANTO DAIME

I was thinking about doing jungle tours, and taking people out to do ayahuasca, to experience it in a jungle setting. I set out to get to know the Santo Daime and the União do Vegetal groups, two Brazilian religions that use ayahuasca in their ceremonies. A student connected me to the Santo Daime group first, and they invited me to one of their ceremonial centers a couple of hours outside Manaus. It was a beautiful property, nestled in the jungle, bordering a lake. Probably sixty or eighty people had gathered for the ceremony, ranging from teenagers to elders.

It seemed promising, but the ceremony itself was nothing like I expected. I have never been overly receptive to religion, and this ceremony came across as an intense religious service. It actually felt cultish to me.

The Santo Daime have created a merger between Christianity and ayahuasca, which they call Daime. They use the medicine as a sacrament to connect them to God. During the ceremony, the participants wear all-white costumes and the women stand separately from the men. Everyone gets a special hymn book, and they sing and dance together while on the medicine to generate an energy or a connection to God.

They gave me a book, and I had to pretend I was

singing, or at least look at the book and try to sing along. Everybody was doing a sort of two-step dance at the same time. It was worlds apart from my previous experiences, drinking ayahuasca in a dark setting, going quietly into myself in my own space. It felt really strange. Here, people were dancing all around with crazy looks in their eyes and vomiting everywhere. They would go outside and vomit in broad view before going back in and dancing and singing some more.

As the only English-speaking, white guy there, I felt out of place. It was culture shock of a sort. Any time I sat down to regroup, one of the organizers would grab me and push me to sing and dance. Even when I tried to find a secluded spot to purge, people kept coming to get me and dragging me back into the strange phenomenon unfolding inside the ceremonial space. Everyone was extremely welcoming, but the overall scene was not my cup of tea.

During the ceremony, I was hoping my friend Lawrence would show up. I met him at the hostel earlier in the year—he worked there—and he had told me he was thinking of trying ayahuasca to address some problems in his life. We talked a lot. He told me he felt like he was participating in a lot of self-destructive behaviors, like drinking and getting into fights, even playing in traffic. He confessed he felt like a demon was controlling his life and putting him in danger. He was afraid he might kill himself, and he wanted to spare his one-year-old son that pain.

He was originally going to drive me to the Santo Daime ceremony and stay with me. As of Tuesday that week, we were planning it out, but by Thursday, I couldn't get hold of him. It was the same on Friday, and the ceremony was set for Saturday. I assumed that he had gotten nervous about going, but I never heard a word.

By the time I returned on Sunday, I still hadn't heard from him and I started mentally berating him. I thought, *This guy, what a jerk to ditch me like that.* The next day, though, I learned the truth. Lawrence had died in a car crash on the Avenida do Turismo on Wednesday night. Alcohol was probably a factor. They had a funeral and buried him the next day, closed casket.

Lawrence's death had a huge impact on me. I had just been talking to him a few days before, listening to him tell me how much he wanted to live. And now, he was gone. His death spurred me to completely quit drinking alcohol. For the rest of my stay in Brazil, I didn't touch a drop.

It was surprisingly easy to stop. I came from a culture where alcohol is essentially the only recreational activity available. In rural Canada, people drink at work, they drink after work, and they get really drunk on the weekend. I had been drinking regularly for a decade or more and I got plastered just about every weekend. I was nervous about weekends without drinking. I hadn't socialized without a drink in my hand since high school. Could I really just stop?

UNIÃO DO VEGETAL

After the Santo Daime ceremony, I started doing ceremonies with another group, the União do Vegetal (UDV). Somehow, I was able to hang out with these folks without drinking. When I finished a weekend there, I would feel really good, not sick and hungover.

UDV ceremonies felt better to me than the Santo Daime rituals. Even though the religious aspect remained, the UDV didn't focus so much on Christianity as spirituality. They talked about God, but nobody handed me a hymn book or wove Bible stories into their discourse like the Santo Daime did.

The group was building a big, new ceremonial structure, so they would get together to work on it, then have a meal, with the kids all running around playing before the ceremony started. During the ceremony, elders sat at a central table, and they would drink first. Then they invited everyone else to get their cup of "Vegetal," which is what the UDV called their sacrament.

I sat in a comfortable chair in a well-lit space. Music and song filled the room, but it was gentle and contemplative. I never felt forced to join in the singing. I felt much more at home in this place and with these people. Everyone was helpful, offering rides home after the ceremony, even at four or five o'clock in the morning. I made some good friends there and went back to see them in 2014 when I organized the Brazil World Cup Ayahuasca Adventure.

I didn't necessarily recognize that I was filing away ideas for my own future from these ceremonies, but the way ayahuasca practice works, you stop looking at it like individual ceremonies. The practice becomes an ongoing process rather than a series of encounters. Often, the first ceremony feels like a huge event because you make rapid progress. As time goes on, each occasion functions more like a check-in, giving you a chance to reset yourself.

I managed to extend my visa, so I spent a couple of months in Manaus before returning to Canada for a friend's wedding and to see about working for my dad again. He was on board with Tim Ferriss's ideas about remote work, so I didn't have to actually be sitting in the small town of Walkerton. I could travel and work, attend meetings, and follow up on sales calls from the road.

Meanwhile, education was high on my agenda. I hated not having any qualifications. I kept going back to sales because I hit roadblocks everywhere else, and I needed to open up some other options.

My dad supported me in pursuing higher education, which was helpful. In April 2012, he found Royal Roads University, which offered a flexible admissions process that allowed me to use life experience to gain acceptance. It was the perfect place for someone like me.

STORIES OF PERSONAL TRANSFORMATION:
GUY CRITTENDEN

An environmental journalist and writer, Guy Crittenden talks about what makes ayahuasca so transformative and how his experiences at Pulse Tours and Ayahuasca Adventure Center have helped him discover his mission in life. Look for more from Guy on Blogspot, his writings on the Pulse Tours website, and in his forthcoming book, *The Year of Drinking Magic: 12 Ceremonies with the Vine of Souls.*

"I only ever consciously thought of myself as being on a spiritual path, probably within the past seven or eight years. I suppose you could say it went back ten years to when I separated from my wife at the time. I went through a period when I was very rudderless. I was working as an editor and writer for a couple of environmental magazines that at one time I'd owned with a couple of partners and we sold to a conglomerate. My career was the only thing that was stable in my life after I got divorced. I spent a couple of years in and out of relationships, exploring the nightlife of Toronto, doing all the wild and crazy things that I couldn't do when I was married. It was very hedonistic, and I wouldn't say it would qualify as spiritual in most people's books. There is an element of any spiritual journey where one explores one's shadow. I now view that rudderless period as a period of exploring my shadow self.

I was doing shadow work, although I wouldn't have had the vocabulary then to call it that.

"Then I was listening to the radio one day and I heard an interview on Canadian Public Radio on a program that focuses on spirituality. The host was interviewing a fellow by the name of Brad Warner, who is a punk rock bass player and also an ordained Soto school Zen monk. He was talking about a book that he'd written about meditation with the memorable name *Sit Down and Shut Up*, which despite its catchy name is actually an explication of the work of thirteenth-century Zen monk Dōgen, who is to Zen Buddhism what Shakespeare is to English literature. That put me into a path of several years of studying Buddhism and starting a meditation practice, and through that, I was led to the insight that I only got at that time on an intellectual level, not an experiential level, that what we are, each of us, are local manifestations of a universal nonlocal consciousness. Or as Ram Dass puts it rather humorously, we are all God in drag. God in disguise. God hiding from himself, pretending he's not himself, which is a foundational idea of Hinduism and Buddhism.

"I was on that path when I came across a little video that showed people on a trip in the Amazon. I liked two aspects of what was being offered by this little travel company called Pulse Tours. One aspect was that I could go to the Amazon, which is to environmentalists what the Vatican is to Catholics, so I could genuflect to my espoused interest in the environment, but I could also go and drink ayahuasca three times at a shamanic retreat center. I called Dan Cleland. It was hard to get a hold of anyone at Pulse because Dan and Tatyana were away leading a tour. Eventually, I heard back from them and I arranged to join their ten-day trip over New Year's Eve of 2013–2014. That's how it all came to be.

"My experience with psychedelics was at that time limited to just one experience that I had when I was in my twenties. I'd been on a hiking trip with a couple of guys in the Adirondack Mountains, and one of them, who's a cousin of mine, had brought along some LSD in blotter form. I had an experience with that that made a great impression on me. In fact, given how beautiful and profound that experience was, it's amazing to me that I didn't do it again. In that experience, I'd developed a godlike or superpower of hearing and I could hear every bird, plant, and insect for miles. Not only could I hear them all, but I could also track what each one was up to individually rather than as a big cacophony. That changed my perception of reality because I realized at that moment that our normal state of consciousness is highly filtered and that what a lot of our brain is doing is not so much bringing in information as it is filtering it out so that as the hunter-gatherers that we evolved from, we could concentrate on a much narrower band of experience that allowed us to be successful hunters and allowed us to hunt food and not become food.

"Then I fell back into my life and I got busy with my career and getting married and starting a family and all that. It was only when my marriage ended and my children were older that I got back onto this thing that I call my past. Because of the LSD experience, I had this kind of dormant interest in psychedelics, but our culture always presents these things as drugs and it always presents them as taboos. Unless you're moving in certain crowds, which I was not moving in for a long time, they're not easy to come by. One of the problems with LSD for a very long time, and I know this from people who were moving in the right crowds, is it's not easy to come by good LSD. I would have had to go way out of my way to find it at a time when I was busy with other things.

"That all changed when the movement got under way. I think it is a movement, which we could call the psychedelic movement, or the new psychedelic movement, which is like the psychedelic movement of the counterculture of the 1960s and '70s. Except unlike that, it's based in the shamanic or the teacher plants or the master plants. Once I started looking into that further, I realize it would not be difficult to have an experience in a really good context. With psychedelics, set and setting are important. With ayahuasca in the better centers, everything is set up in your favor to experience it in a safe container, so to speak.

"So, I finally bought my ticket and I took my turn. I was not sure what to expect at that time and it's funny to think it was only three or four years ago. There was not the robust amount of information and personal accounts available that there are today. I remember browsing the Internet and reading everything I could to try and get a handle on what my experience might be. People would talk about seeing geometry and colors, but it seems that there were not a lot of good writers at that time. I didn't really know what to expect, but the first night we drank... Well, it takes about thirty or forty minutes for the medicine to come on and for the DMT to cross into the blood-brain barrier. Within only a few minutes of that happening, this reality was completely switched out for another reality.

"I know that some of the other people on the trip didn't have much in the way of visions or teachings. A lot of them had more of a feeling of the medicine cleaning them out in terms of their digestion and stuff. My experience was, I was dropped right into the deep end of the swimming pool and had an extremely profound visionary experience or sequence of visionary experiences that are pretty much as good as it could get. I'm very sensitive to these medicines and I respond very powerfully to them. That's not an accident. I found almost right away that I was experiencing an alternate dimension of reality that was as people like Terence McKenna describe it; it was extraordinary in its accuracy, its detail, and its clarity.

"One of the things I'd wondered before I did it was, was it going to feel like a dream and was I going to be put in a temporarily psychotic state in which I would mistake my dreams for reality. The DMT chemical is the same chemical that is implicated in our dreaming and in the visions of near-death experiences (NDEs). What I found was that that other dimension was more real than real. I was shocked at the precision of the visions. The visions looked like they were made from etched glass or with the detail of a Fabergé egg. Everything was crusted with jewels, luminescent. Everything moving. I just went on a wild carpet ride, a magic carpet ride to many, many experiences in that one first night. Many hundreds of teachings, some of them more memorable than others. My entire sense of reality was permanently changed on that first night. Then the other two nights that I drank ayahuasca down there just further confirmed that. My entire world changed on that trip.

"Subsequently, I have drunk ayahuasca about fifteen times. I have begun to explore other plant medicines like San Pedro cactus, which is also known as huachuma, and certain other, more subtle plants. I've also started to use psilocybin mushrooms. Always, I might add, in a reverential and ceremonial type of context. I don't use them as a recreational or party drug, so to speak. I'm always amazed when people tell me that they went to a party and they took mushrooms and they had all kinds of shits and giggles because I can't do that. The way that I resonate with those teacher plants is I am, even at a low dose, immediately transported into that other dimension. It usually starts with a lot of lessons in humility, and if there's anything less than reverential in my attitude, I have my ass handed to me.

"Now I feel that I have been called to a shamanic path myself and I'm in the process of figuring out what that means in the context of living in a modern technocratic society. I know some people go to South America and they drink ayahuasca or they experience huachuma or one of these plants and they do it two or three times and then they come back to their life in North America and they just go back to their life. They say, well, that was my experience. They might have got some benefit out of it. They might feel like they got the equivalent of a couple of years of psychiatry in one night. It might help them resolve questions they have about a career path or a relationship they're in and things like that.

"Some other people respond to these experiences so powerfully that they actually go back to South America or they stay there and they serve an apprenticeship with a shaman. They either move permanently to South America or they're there for six months or a year and then they bring those skills back to whatever their home country is, in North America or Europe. My path seems to be a bit different than that. I seem to be called to establish a beachhead, like an early invasion force of the invasion of Normandy in World War II, to establish or revive Celtic shamanism in North America. There's something that is calling me and I've been resisting it, but it keeps calling me back and it keeps bringing me back in.

"Curiously, I went to South America expecting to drink ayahuasca, which I guess was all about just experiencing that plant. Yet surprisingly, it has changed my life and I now find myself on a very unexpected path that has a lot less to do with ayahuasca and a lot more to do with shamanism. In other words, that plant is just one of several plants that are part of the shamanic toolbox. For me, it's not about ayahuasca anymore. It's about shamanism and that can involve plants and sometimes not involve plants.

"I don't know what my shamanic path will look like yet. Last year, I quit my job of twenty-five years. I was ready to move on. I would have left the job in a few years anyway, but my experience with Pulse Tours inspired me to move that date forward on my calendar and get on with it.

"I'd been a magazine editor and writer for twenty-five years. My partners and I started a publication on pollution control in 1989, and a couple of years later, we had started a magazine on waste management and recycling. I was ready to move on, so now I do freelance writing. My themes are still environmental protection, but now I also write about spirituality and shamanism. What I'm especially interested in is where those things intersect. In other words, there are some writers who write about shamanism or spirituality and there are some writers who write about environmental protection, but there are not a lot of writers who are bringing all of that together.

"The solution to our environmental challenges requires a consciousness shift. Otherwise, if all we're doing is worrying about what kind of plastic bottle we can throw in our recycling bin, it's like rearranging the deck chairs on the *Titanic*. The level of transformation that has to take place in society for us to turn the juggernaut around, to continue that metaphor, is significant and it's not going to be supplied by the ego, mind, and the male-dominated culture that we've been trapped in for hundreds of years, especially since the beginning of the Industrial Revolution.

"I actually have come to believe that shamanism and the teacher plants are integral to the changes that are happening and the consciousness shift that's already under way. Essentially, our culture is being assaulted—and I use that term positively—from an angle that it was completely unprepared for, and that is the male dominator, imperialistic, colonial culture that we're still in. We're being broadsided by these master plants and shamanic traditions that channel a very feminine energy and connect us directly to what we could call the Gaian mind. That's where I'm at now and that's what I'm working at trying to understand and trying to promote through my work and my writing. Yeah, I got a lot out of my Pulse Tours experience.

"Dan and Pulse Tours are doing some very interesting

work with their Ayahuasca Adventure Center. What he's building there is very much a fusion of some different styles of personal transformation. I think he's carved out an interesting niche where he's properly understood that what we experienced with the ayahuasca medicine is a revival of what had been a dying or fading indigenous custom. Back when Terence McKenna and the other hippies of the '70s and '60s were going to South America, it was very difficult to find ayahuasca. It was very difficult to find a shaman who knew where to and how to prepare the medicine. This was a tradition that was in steep decline.

"People are sometimes very critical of how it's being exploited now and there's some foundation for that. The tourism around spiritual and therapeutic use of this medicine is actually what has revived it and it's now going out into the broader culture. What is needed or one of several things that is needed is opportunities for people to use that or harness the power of ayahuasca to slingshot themselves into more rapid and powerful personal transformations. When we go to the center, people can do all kinds of exercise—they can do martial arts training and all this kind of stuff—and also have trips out into the jungle and trying to reflect about what they're doing. There are different styles of other types of centers that are needed, too, but Dan is filling a really good niche.

"What I have been shown on the medicine...I don't even know if Dan realizes this yet. I did tell him one time, and

I do think it's going to happen, is that not only will he be part of bringing spiritual seekers to South America to heal themselves, but I think he's going to be involved in the next level, which is to start training shamans. I think his ayahuasca retreat center could eventually become like a Shaolin Temple where people come and get specific training and then they would be sent back to North America to extend teachings of the plants into the technocratic societies that are actually pulling down the Amazon and every major ecosystem in the world. It's like the plant, the spirit of the jungle is spreading her vines around the world herself and she's using that other network of the Internet to do that."

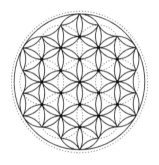

CHAPTER THREE

THE CLASSROOM OF LIFE

THE YEARS 2012 THROUGH 2014 WERE HUGE GROWTH years for me. Taking Tim Ferriss's advice to "work to learn, not work to earn," I combined school, work, and entrepreneurial adventure in the launch of Pulse Tours and Ayahuasca Adventure Center. We ran the first official Pulse tour in December 2011, after which I went to work for an incredible mentor at an international sales and marketing company and worked toward my master's degree. All the hard work began to pay off as Pulse hit the Internet and interest exploded.

During this period, I started working with Simon Sinek's *Start with Why* book, doing the exercises he recommends when making decisions. I would make spreadsheets with two columns; one might list "Thirty things I like about Vancouver" while another compiled "Thirty reasons why I'm working at ZAG." Each day for a month, I wrote down one new item in each column. I did the same thing when I started my master's degree. Having these reasons written down was invaluable; I referred to them more than once when the going got tough.

READY TO LAUNCH

In December 2011, I put together a Panama tour for my sister Catherine and her friends. I ran the tour, executed the itinerary, and handled the budget. I didn't make profit on this trip, but I gained significant experience. Planning the excursion taught me how to estimate expenses, deal with budget spreadsheets, and cope when things changed, as they inevitably do.

First, though, I needed a name for this adventure. I remembered trip titles from my G Adventures days, things like "The Costa Rica Adventure" or "The Panama Experience," but I wanted something that indicated the energy of our enterprise and the vibrancy of our itinerary. That's how the virgin expedition of Pulse Tours came to be known as The Panama Pulse.

I created a pitch for the tour, complete with enticing photographs and engaging descriptions. It seemed right to use the word *pulse*, which described the excitement, energy, and activity I was looking for. The trip was very energetic, involving a catamaran tour, surfing, hiking in the cloud forests, a New Year's Eve party in Bocas del Toro, and even more nightlife in Panama City. We started as Pulse Custom Tours and created the first version of our logo—with an image of an electrical pulse readout—a graphical element we still use today.

The trip itself was a hit. The group, nicknamed Team Extreme, had a great experience, drank a lot of rum, and developed lifelong friendships.

There was no ayahuasca involved in this first trip, but a year later, I was ready to combine the spiritual adventure with the physical one. I was looking at the date of December 12, 2012, along with many watching the Mayan calendar wind down, not as the "end of the world" but as a new beginning. It seemed an auspicious time to launch my first tour that included ayahuasca in the itinerary.

I called this one the Pulse of the Shaman tour and went all out with advertising and developing the Pulse brand. I created a website, set up a PayPal account, debuted on Facebook, and started featuring reviews of the Panama Pulse tour on the site.

Reviews were important in the early going. I ran the trip with only a few people, knowing I would lose money but gain credibility. I understood that incremental growth was an important foundation for sustainable growth.

The Pulse of the Shaman tour was a two-week journey starting in Bogotá, Colombia, traveling by air to the border town of Leticia, and taking a river speedboat up the

Amazon to Iquitos. We did a small jungle tour in Leticia. The main event, however, was a series of ceremonies we held in a center that was new to us. It was a Shipibo-style center with a well-kept, circular ceremonial building. This spot became one of our favorite places to experience the medicine. The event itself was a more vibrant experience than the Chavin ceremony at Shimbre, with two or three singing shamans adding a rich sonic dimension to the proceedings. The songs had a piercing quality, and the shaman touched on the Mayan doomsday prophecy that was on everyone's mind. They served fresh, strong medicine as five or more people—the shamans and the apprentices—sang their icaros at the same time, building up the sonic layers and the energy in the building. It felt like the roof was about to pop off.

It was a visceral experience and a powerful, transformative reminder of the power of ayahuasca. I gained insight into ways to make changes in my health going forward and met Wiler, the shaman who would ultimately come to work at the Ayahuasca Adventure Center.

Everyone had similarly satisfying experiences, saying, "Wow, this stuff really works." Their reactions reaffirmed my dedication to combining travel and ayahuasca and finding a good-quality center to work with.

The ceremony ended around midnight, and we were picked up on three-wheeled dirt bikes at three or four in the morning so we could make it to our "Greyhound of the water"—an Amazon speedboat—at dawn. The twelve-hour ride to Leticia left plenty of time for contemplation, and I reflected on how important ayahuasca is to being human. I rediscovered my belief that every human should experience at least once this profound awareness of all of humanity, the great, awe-inspiring mystery of it all. I had kind of forgotten the depth of the meditative psychedelic state between ceremonies. This trip had been just the reminder I needed. It encouraged me to believe in what I was doing, that this work could have life-changing, transformative power. It gave me renewed motivation and passion for Pulse Tours.

We traced our route back down the Amazon to Leticia, then to Bogotá where everyone caught their flights home. I landed back in Toronto, where we would set the stage for our breakthrough moment to come in June.

WORK TO LEARN

Fresh off that trip, I dived into my master's studies and started working closely with Steve Curtis, the founder of ZAG Group, Inc., an online marketing company specializing in ethnobotanicals such as kratom, *salvia divinorum*, kava, and *amanita muscaria* mushrooms. My title had a nice ring to it—international account manager, Europe—and I appreciated the travel opportunities, plus salary and commissions, that came my way, but I was most interested in Steve's mentorship. I wanted to soak up everything I could from this dynamic, successful entrepreneur.

There was so much I wanted to know—how to be an entrepreneur, how to run a business, and how likely it was that my business idea would succeed. Steve knew what I was up to; we had an agreement that I could moonlight in my own business while working for him.

Moonlighting doesn't quite cover the flurry of activity that followed in the business that spring. I worked endlessly, it seemed, gathering testimonials, improving the website, and trying my hand at online advertising. Around this time, a friend in Vancouver suggested I try Reddit. Little did I know what opening myself up to an Ask Me Anything (AMA) session on this active social media site would mean. I shot a short video and posted a teaser: "I take people deep into the heart of the Amazon. Ask me anything."

The AMA blew up. I was glued to the computer answering questions from everywhere. People wanted to know everything from the various brews and mixtures of ayahuasca to what I knew about the problems at the Shimbre center, where a participant had died. (Shimbre's program was not safe for all participants. Untrained people should not have been left alone to endure the medicine without access to support and proper bathrooms. In the middle of the jungle, any number of threats could be present, from snakes and spiders to jaguars. Their experience made us insist that our programs would be safe, our guests would be cared for, and our facilities would be accessible.)

Getting more than six hundred comments and becoming the top search result on Reddit showed us how much interest there was in what we were building. For the first time, I got inquiries from people who didn't know me at all. The amount of information I provided in that AMA showed people they could trust me and our process. We booked ten people on the next trip immediately.

STRONG PULSE

The June tour involved the same itinerary as the December Pulse of the Shaman tour, but there was a greater cohesiveness to this group. We had eight passengers from the Reddit community, plus me and Tatyana, and we quickly became a family. The travel portion of the tour helped us to bond as a kind of tribe before we ever set foot in the ceremonial space. Preceremony bonding was something that hadn't been done elsewhere. The camaraderie made us braver; if anything went wrong, everyone knew they had someone alongside them to offer a helping hand.

The trip went off without a hitch. The feedback we got was fulfilling: one passenger thanked us for helping him get back a part of himself he thought was lost forever, and another told us the trip had revived his spark and helped him recover from grief over losing some close friends. If we wanted proof of concept, this was it. This thing worked.

GETTING TOGETHER

Most satisfying of all, many of the relationships developed on this trip have lasted to this day, including mine with Tatyana. We had met through Facebook, where we were attracted to each other's profiles. I knew Tatyana had lived in Colombia and knew Spanish. Plus, she was thinking about quitting her job and working in a more spiritual realm. We started talking about working together but were both a bit shy about it before the June tour.

During the June ceremony, though, we both received strong messages about each other. Tatyana appeared in my visions, along with the message that I needed to "do something now." We had our first kiss after the second ceremony of the session, on the balcony outside the maloca. Ayahuasca had told me that Tatyana was the one I should be with, and when I saw her standing there, draped in white, I felt emboldened by the medicine to take a chance. We have been partners in a variety of ways ever since.

BACK IN BUSINESS

Meanwhile, I was still involved with ZAG, which was expanding quickly. Growing pains were inevitable in a company that went from making seven figures a year to seven figures a month, but the dysfunctional management reaffirmed my distaste for being at the mercy of my "superiors." I didn't want to conform or obey; I wanted to create. I still needed the paycheck, though, so I spent my time off investing in marketing, building the website, and developing new tours for Pulse. I saw Pulse as a glowing ember that needed tending, so I probably would have left my corporate job sooner or later, but a personality clash with the CFO hastened my progress toward the exit door. In September, I handed in my resignation. That was the last time I ever worked for someone else.

My quality of life improved dramatically once I started focusing on my own projects. Entrepreneurs deal with anxiety and stress all the time, but being the owner of the outcome makes a world of difference. You start to see the work as your baby. You're responsible for caring for it, and then you watch it mature.

We were in for a big growth spurt in 2013, with three trips organized for one month alone, while I was still finishing up my master's degree. My field study took me to China, where the pollution knocked me for a loop, healthwise. I went from the pristine air of Canada to smog-filled cities like Beijing, Jinan, and Qufu. Beijing and Qufu were bad, but the absolute worst was Jinan. Jinan is about the size of New York City and had absorbed much of the industry that had moved north from Beijing to make way for the Olympics. The daily smog warnings were off the charts, often coded in the red "hazardous" zone with airborne particulate matter well over five hundred parts per million. I couldn't see across the street. A fierce cough persisted throughout the three weeks I spent there; even with the heavy-duty antibiotics I took, I coughed up blood each morning. It was certainly educational but perhaps not in the way my school intended.

Happily, I was scheduled to be back in Colombia after this, with Tatyana, to launch the Mother of All Adventures tour, which would ultimately deliver us to the beautiful village of Libertad, Peru. Here, we would meet Ricardo, who would become a guide on many trips for us.

My father and uncle came with us on part of the Mother tour, along with Michael Sanders, Guy Crittenden, travelers from Lithuania and Norway, and others. The twenty-two-day trip had two legs. The first took us through Colombia and included a jungle tour and retreat in Iquitos. The second part took us to Lima, Peru, where we explored the ancient Inca architecture at Machu Picchu and participated in a ceremony with San Pedro, another sacred plant medicine. We then traveled to Cusco to see the Inca ruins and visited a different ayahuasca center in Puerto Maldonado during this trip. After this retreat, Michael Sanders ended up writing an entire book, *Ayahuasca: An Executive's Enlightenment,* about his ayahuasca experiences.

We were having various time line and financial issues with this facility, which only reaffirmed the certainty growing in my mind: we needed to start our own center.

The June Solstice Journey had garnered a lot of attention on Reddit. The tour filled up quickly with people outside my personal network for the first time. I was still in guerrilla marketing mode until this point, leaving posters at shops like Urban Shaman in Vancouver, making lots of posts on social media, commenting in online forums, and networking. At one point, Tatyana and I even walked the streets of Toronto, stapling posters up on telephone poles and bulletin boards. None of that came close to the volume we received through Aya Advisors. After the trip, Pulse Tours was number one on the Aya Advisors website for two years straight and things turned around in a big way.

By the time New Year's Eve rolled around, it was evident that the business could potentially be sustainable. We took our first eight-day tour to and from Iquitos and started planning what was to come in the new year.

STORIES OF PERSONAL TRANSFORMATION:
TATYANA TELEGINA

I met Tatyana Telegina in June 2013 on the June Solstice Journey. We joined forces then and have been building Pulse Tours and Ayahuasca Adventure Center as a team ever since. Originally from Almaty, Kazakhstan, Tatyana has a multicultural background; she has lived in Colombia, Kazakhstan, Montreal, and Toronto. She speaks four languages fluently (Spanish, English, French, and Russian). She shares her personal and professional story here.

"Before I discovered ayahuasca and got involved with Pulse Tours, I was working in IT in the sales department. It definitely wasn't the type of a job where I felt like I was fulfilling my life's purpose. It was [just] there. At one point, my friend told me about this urban shaman who was in Toronto. That's where I've lived for many, many years.

"I was really curious because I had heard about ayahuasca, but I thought that it was only possible to do it in Peru. To find out that it was actually available in Toronto definitely sparked my interest. I decided to try it out because there was an upcoming ceremony with that same urban shaman that my friend was telling me about, and so I went for it.

"I did my first ayahuasca ceremony in Toronto in 2012. I had a very smooth ceremony. I had a lot of fear going into it, but something inside of me was telling me that there's absolutely nothing to worry about and everything is going to be OK. That's exactly how it was. It was very smooth. It was very full of light and lots of really beautiful insights.

"I think this is where it started through me personally [with] ayahuasca and I think eventually this was also something that led me to Pulse and to Dan and to where I am right now with my life. I did two more ceremonies with that same urban shaman and it was a completely different experience from what people experience when they come to the jungles of Peru and actually do it in a ceremonial context with shamans who sing icaros, the healing songs.

"It was still good experience. It was still very opening to me especially at that time. That actually led me to quitting my job in IT because it opened me up so much on so many levels. It just showed me that life is a beautiful thing, and I know that I have a lot of inner potential and healing capabilities and I definitely want to do something different than IT in my life. That actually made me quit my job because I physically couldn't be there anymore. I was going to work and I couldn't work. Literally, my body was just not moving.

"I thought, *You know what? This is clear. Very, very clear that I need to quit.* I had some money saved up, so I wanted to just go and do some soul searching and do a little bit of traveling.

"I put together an itinerary for myself which included a month in the jungle to do a plant diet or to try ayahuasca. Before going into the jungle, I met Dan, through Facebook. He posted in an ayahuasca group about this tour that he was organizing, the June Solstice 2013 tour. He had a website with the map and all the details and I was like, 'Wow, this sounds amazing.'

"I thought it sounded perfect, to go and do ayahuasca in Peru with a tour leader and a group of people, traveling before that, seeing all these cool places in Peru and South America. My dates lined up, so I had started with a retreat by myself in Colombia at a family friend's apartment, planning to meet up with Dan and the group after a week.

"I reached out to Dan for details of the trip. We were actually able to work out a pretty good deal for me because he said that he wouldn't mind using some help. I knew a tiny bit of Spanish at that point and I thought, *You know what? That would be awesome.*

"I met Dan for the first time in Bogotá, Colombia, where the trip started. I think we started checking each other out a little bit even before the tour began through Facebook; we probably stalked each other's profiles quite a bit. We liked what we saw, but there was no expectation. We were both interested in just meeting each other in person and seeing how the whole thing developed.

"When I first saw him and he saw me, I think there was definitely a spark of interest between us. We were just connecting regularly on the trip, nothing superspecial, but when we got to the center that Dan at that time was working with, our personal relationship just sparked in a big way.

"During the ceremonies held there, I had visions about Dan. He had visions about me. During the second ceremony out of the three, we just really connected. Mother ayahuasca showed him that he needed to make a move toward me and not waste any more time because this trip might end and we might never see each other again.

"It was a beautiful, beautiful ceremony. It was so rough on me at the beginning, but I got a lot out of it, and toward the end, I just felt so empowered and just so balanced and with a sense of deep, deep peace within me. It was a very beautiful state.

"I remember when I was getting my healing song from the main shaman at that center, when the song was finished, all I wanted to do was just to go and hug Dan. There was nothing else in my mind. As my song finished, I looked toward his mat and I saw that he just got up to go to the bathroom. I got up and I went outside of the maloca.

"That was a beautiful night. Very, very bright, very clear, lots of stars. I was standing there just beside the entrance of the maloca waiting for Dan to come back. As I'm standing there, Melissa [Melissa Stangl, Pulse Tours' director of operations] also comes back into the maloca from the bathroom and she's like, 'Oh, hey. Oh, you're standing here just like Mother Earth covered in your blanket.'

"I didn't realize that Dan was already standing right in front of me. He approached me and just gave me this huge hug. I was like, 'Oh, well, that's exactly what I was going to do.' He hugged me and I hugged him back and it was just like a friendly kind of embrace at first.

"Then at that moment, I just realized I needed to surrender to it and just trust it. I did surrender and actually really embraced him as a woman would embrace a man. That translated into a kiss. That was our first kiss. It was beautiful. That was it.

"It was a beautiful ceremony, and I know that it is not always that way, especially elsewhere in the world like in the United States and Canada, where people called shamans may not be trustworthy. That's why it's really important for people to do their research well when they are deciding to go to Peru and choosing a center.

"It's important to know the history and [do] the research and not just go into any center. Especially do not come to Iquitos and just expect to find a center at the very last minute. It usually doesn't turn out that well. It's good to do research and know exactly what you're getting into.

"I think I got really lucky when I did my three first ceremonies with an urban shaman. I call him an urban shaman, but he's not really a shaman. He's just somebody who knows how to prepare ayahuasca. He's a good guy. He knows a lot about plants and he's a genius in that regard. He has good energies and good intentions, and I think that if people have good intentions, even if they're doing ceremonies on their own like this, outside of Peru, it's a good sign.

"At the same time, if somebody is doing a ceremony without a properly trained shaman, and if they go very deep in their experience and they need a little bit of help and there is no shaman near them, then that could be a little bit challenging and even actually dangerous. Sometimes, especially if people are dealing with deep traumas or they have a lot to release, if they have been using substances or they're very traumatized, ayahuasca can take them very, very deep.

"A lot of the times, it's the deep and the challenging ceremonies that are giving us the most benefit, but not everybody can handle that space. For some people, it might be a little bit too much. If you don't have a shaman who can help you get out of that space, it could actually be a little bit traumatic.

"That's why it's not really recommended to do ceremonies outside of South America unless you really, really know what you're putting yourself into and the person who runs the ceremonies is really truly highly recommended by many people. It's just nicer to come to South America, but I understand that not a lot of people have the financial capabilities of doing that.

"At the Pulse center, we create a safe space through the people who work there. We make a very, very huge emphasis on our staff and on the quality of people whom we employ at the center. We have an amazing team. I'm really saying that from the heart because we're so grateful for them. They're working from the heart and they're loving it. I think if people are doing something that they love that it's hard not to be good at it.

"These guys are really good and they're so connected with the medicine. All of our facilitators, and even other staff, do plant diets [an aspect of shamanic training that involves ingesting special plants or plant extracts for extended periods of time] so they are really connected to the medicine and to the whole shamanic path. At every ceremony they talk about ayahuasca and give our guests different tips on how to navigate the space when they're on the ceremony. It seems like ayahuasca is talking through them. They're just pure channels for the medicine. Even though they are called facilitators, these guys are almost like shamans in their own way.

"The plant diets are definitely used to learn and to better oneself and to learn icaros and how to become a shaman, but they're also used to heal one's body and mind and spirit. Ideally, if people are really trying to cure something and it's something serious, we definitely want them to stay at the center for the longest time possible to try a plant diet and to really get all the benefits from it.

"We put interested guests on custom diets and they heal. One man had diabetes, and we put him on a plant diet with a plant called abuta. He healed himself from diabetes completely. He went home feeling so much better that he wrote an article about it.

"Plants can help with a lot of traumas or conditions. There are particular plants that help people get over addiction. Or if somebody wants to get pregnant, for example, and she can't, there are also plants to help with that. If you have cancer, for example, then there are very powerful plants that you can diet with and that can help you cure that as well. There are definitely a lot of different plants used for just a variety of different things. There are plants that you can diet with that help you heal your anger or get rid of your anger.

"We take our medicine very, very seriously. Our main priority is definitely for people to get as much healing as possible. Another little twist on our center is that we also do jungle expeditions during the day. People can actually learn about the jungle and the animals and the environment that they're around. We have a professional jungle guide who takes them out during the daytime because there are a lot of beautiful things to see, especially in the area where we're at.

"I think Dan and I were chosen for this mission because everything just started unfolding for us. Dan and I continued doing the tours, I had quit my job, and Dan also quit his job so that both of us could focus on the tours way more. We invested a lot of energy into making this happen.

"It wasn't easy at the beginning, but we worked hard. These tours were going pretty well. People were finding us and going on the trips with us. Then at one point, it was so clear that we were into this work, we loved it, and we were pretty good at it. Dan had worked as a tour leader for many, many years, so he knew the territory very well, and I'm so into the medicine. We both dealt with people well and we had an amazing jungle guide.

"The territory where we would take people on the jungle explorations, we knew it well. Basically, we ended up making this agreement with the village [Libertad] and they gave us a piece of land on which to build the center. It had started to be challenging for us to bring people to the other reputable center that we were working with at that time. Either they would have no space when we are ready to book or we would have to let them know too far in advance to make sense for us.

"It was challenging, but at the same time, our tours were going and people were coming. We were like, 'What do we do?' Either we just stop doing what we're doing or move to the next level and build our own center. At that time, we already knew a really good shaman, so everything just aligned itself so perfectly for us. It's like the path was open. I think this is the main reason why ayahuasca brought me and Dan together, for us to create that.

"I feel like when the feminine and the masculine come together, it's very powerful. That's what happened, and we started building the center little by little. The operation was going pretty well and still is. Hopefully will be for many years to come.

"We have a female shaman who works at our center, Angelita. She also sings icaros. She's not the lead shaman, but it's so crucial and important to have that feminine and masculine balance. She is balancing everything so well and she's powerful, but in her own way.

"I have played many roles at Pulse. At the beginning, I was a tour guide. I was a facilitator. I was also doing all the bookings and all the reservations. We had no budget to employ somebody else to do that. Every time you start your own business, it's just like that. You just have to do a lot of work at the beginning. You have to move everything you have into it.

"As we started doing a little bit better and we were able to hire somebody to help us with the facilitation and then eventually we hired Melissa who became our operations manager. Now, she's the one who handles all the e-mails and all the bookings and reservations.

"It was such a relief. It was really busy. We had no weekends. It was just work all the time. It's not a complaint. That's just the way how, I guess, businesses work. You want to start your own thing, you get yourself into something like that.

"It was amazing to have Melissa on board with us when she came. She's just such a gem. She took a huge chunk of work off my shoulders, and I was able to focus more on the guests themselves and actually be with people rather than always running around and making sure everything is good and answering e-mails at the same time.

"At the moment, I'm managing the center, making sure everything runs smoothly. I'm not really facilitating anymore. We have people who are doing that full time and they're superimmersed into it. I started managing things from a bit more of a bird's eye view. There are always lots of different things to do every day. I love it.

"I'm also on a shamanic path myself, working not just with ayahuasca but with other plant medicines like San Pedro. It may sound like a little bit out of this world for a lot of people, but all these medicines, they do have spirits and they're very powerful. It's beautiful to be able to develop that kind of connection with them where you can actually call upon them without doing a ceremony. You feel guided.

"The guidance doesn't always go the way you think it will either. I had a ceremony where my intention was to find love for myself and love for life and a way to be happy with myself without necessarily needing somebody in my life in order to be happy. I thought that, *Oh, well, my ceremony is probably going to be full of love and full of light and ayahuasca is going to embrace me and show me how precious I am.*

"It was nothing like that at all. I thought that my soul was being stolen. Not just that I was dying; I thought that somebody was stealing my soul and my soul was going to be stuck somewhere in between dimensions. Some kind of entity was just going to steal my soul and leave my body, pretending that it's me. It was that terrifying.

"It seems like you are dying and somebody should help you, but really the medicine has an intention with you there. When the ceremony was over, I had so much sincere gratitude for the fact that I am here in my body, my soul is here, and I am alive. Basically, through the ceremony, my intention got fulfilled. If I was to just get a nice, easy, loving ceremony, I would have probably forgotten about it maybe in a month's time and that's it. Because the ceremony was so intense and I really had to go through hell, once I got out of it, I had this appreciation for life and for myself. I totally did not need anybody in that moment.

"Most of the time, the most challenging ceremonies are the most rewarding ones actually.

"The rewards of working at the center, though, they come every day. It's definitely nice to meet people from all different parts of the world. Pretty much every week, we have a new group of people that comes in and they're from different parts of the world and from different walks of life. It's incredible because through this work, we now have so many friends all around the world. I think we can basically go anywhere we want and we will have somebody to meet us there, which is really nice.

"It's incredible to be able to help people. I think that's the most fulfilling part of this job. All of the challenges that might arise, every once in a while, it's worth it. You see people and you understand the healing that you are able to facilitate for them. You have a tremendous sense of joy out of that because you know you're doing something important for the world.

"Also, living here is just really good. Just to be in the space and to live in the jungle. As challenging as it is, because it is the jungle and the conditions are pretty rustic, it's still nice because it's very simple. You're able to appreciate the simple things in life. It's nice sometimes to be disconnected from the Internet and sit in the hammock and do nothing. It's not being lazy; it's actually being present in the moment instead of just always running around and doing all these things chasing God knows what.

"It's kind of like a simple life, but it's very fulfilling on many levels. Of course, when you go back home to Canada, you just appreciate your family and hot showers and food and whole foods, so much more. There's definitely a sense of gratitude for what we have back home that arose from this work that we're doing."

PART TWO

—

IGNITION

CHAPTER FOUR

LAUNCH

OUR BUSINESS AT PULSE TOURS AND AYAHUASCA Adventure Center is really not much different than any business, except that we have the added layer of social entrepreneurship. What is social entrepreneurship? Essentially, the social enterprise is an enterprise that is not solely focused on maximizing profits. In a socially progressive company, there are other objectives that are very important to the business.

On a microscale, we work with individual people who come to us for healing and life transformations. In that context, my objective is to improve people's lives or facilitate their transformation. I'm there to help promote personal change.

On a macroscale, our goals are to improve the lives of

the local villagers in Libertad and support conservation efforts for the Amazon jungle. We contribute by donating to Amazon conservation agencies, and we also create economic opportunities. People living near us can work in the ecotourism and hospitality sectors instead of cutting down trees and killing animals for money.

In addition to that, we're working on a renewable energy project in the village, and we make it easier for donations to reach the village. The people in Libertad talk to us about what they need, and we help make that happen. Most of the donations end up going to the school and the children. That's an example of social entrepreneurship in our context.

The happiness quotient in Libertad has gone up significantly because the people now have hope that they can work. We're the largest employer in the village by far, so they certainly appreciate everything we're doing for them. They're very nice people. If you walk through Libertad as one of our guests, everybody will know you. They will wave and smile. It's a friendly relationship.

LESSONS LEARNED

By the time we set up the center in Libertad, a lot of things had come together that hadn't been in place back when I was trying to set up shop in Brazil. I had an established tour business and had already done ten or more trips before actually building the center. I'd also done the exploratory groundwork for the intercultural communication center I had wanted to build in Manaus. Rave reviews and top ratings continued, so we had strong proof of concept going for us, too.

One less tangible factor in the business's success was completing my master's degree. Now I had proof that I could stick with something for the long haul; it made a strong addition to my résumé. What's more, finishing an advanced research project while working full time gave me the confidence I needed. It also made my father more open to investing in my business. He saw how challenging those two years were for me, and how I had worked through it all. He not only had a new faith in my level of commitment, but he also knew that in the worst-case scenario—if the plan didn't work out—I would be able to get a professional job if I needed to.

The worst case was that my plan would fail, I would lose the $25,000 my father loaned me, and I would have to pay it off by going back to North America and getting a high-paying job. I was willing to risk it, and my father was, too. We actually became quite close after I started working with ayahuasca; it opened up our communications. I put everything on the table now; there's no hiding anything. My father was aware of everything that was going on with me.

Not only was our relationship more stable than ever, all signs pointed to the likely success of our ayahuasca endeavor. The business was stable and growing, our concept was unique and well received, and the market was clearly there.

My initial plan was to raise funds through crowdfunding and building relationships with investors. It turned out we didn't have time to roll the project out that gradually, though. By June 2014, we realized we had no home for our September retreat. While we were in Brazil for the World Cup, we were also facing a big decision: build this thing now or look for alternatives.

Along with Tatyana and Ricardo, I put together the case that we needed to do this now and presented it to my father. There was virtually no hesitation; he wanted to see me succeed. He had seen how hard I worked to get to this point, and how many times I had rebounded after getting knocked down, so he was happy to put his money behind the project.

GETTING TO KNOW YOU

With financing secured, I went back down to Peru in mid-July. Ricardo had previously introduced me to Libertad's village president in March, so we already had a tentative agreement.

Libertad is a sweet little gem in the middle of the jungle. Life there is economically basic, but the people have everything they need. It's a tiny place, with about 275 residents whose homes are organized around a grassy central square. Multiple generations of several families live there, often under the same roof.

They catch fish in the river and cultivate rice and yucca in the rich, fertile mud of the riverbanks that twist for thousands of miles down the mountain to concentrate rich nutrients at the bottom. In the summer, also known as low-water season, the villagers can go out and throw rice down in the big mounds of mud and within six months, it's ready to harvest.

When you walk around Libertad, you see smiles everywhere. The adults work together as a village and the children run around playing together. The children are extremely sweet. They may not have a lot in material terms, but they have a deep sense of community that sustains them. Everybody knows everybody else, so they don't have a lot of problems in the village. There's no crime, no visible squalor or suffering. Everybody has a place to live even if it's just a small, square house outfitted with a hammock and a mosquito net. We got really lucky to be able to build a relationship with this village.

In July, we met again with the president and held a couple of town hall meetings with the villagers. The people of Libertad don't actually own the land—it's not a legally registered property according to the Peruvian government—but they have tenure over it. Essentially, what they say goes. So we held several town hall meetings where we explained our intentions and offered up opportunities for the villagers to work construction, clear brush and weeds from the land, and harvest wood for construction. An agreement was reached, based on our ability to provide Libertad's people with ongoing employment and financial aid. We're also working on a solar power project and an English education program. We would love to find someone who wants to come down and live in the jungle to teach English. (If you'd like to send your résumé, the place to do it is changetheworld@pulsetours.com. Please only apply if you have significant experience teaching and are fluent in both Spanish and English.)

Our relationship with the village is ongoing. We help with practical matters, like procuring a water tank for the school, and we support town events and celebrations. They celebrate four big holidays each year: Village Founding Anniversary, Christmas, New Year's, and Mother's Day. For each of these, we contribute a cookout where we barbecue meat and buy the kids some treats. For Christmas, they have a custom of making chocolate milk in a big cauldron. We buy ingredients for that. We bring in fireworks at New Year's and contribute gift baskets stuffed with foods for Mother's Day.

In addition to holidays, we are involved in the everyday life of the village. Each month, we give a contribution toward the monthly public works project that the whole village participates in. When the village holds craft fairs— the women sell artwork, jewelry, carvings, and weavings

made from jungle materials like seeds, beans, and fibers—
we bring our guests over to enjoy the activities and browse
the offerings. These events work both ways: the village
women earn a little money and our guests get to experience village life a little more closely.

Overall, we have been extremely fortunate working
with these folks. In the beginning, when we weren't so
familiar with each other, we may have had a couple of
minor issues, but ultimately, the relationship has been
extremely smooth. Any employer in the Western world
would be jealous of the quality of people who are working
for us from this village.

A big part of our success is due to one villager in particular, Carlos Canayo. Carlos is our right-hand man and
has become like a brother to me over time. Right from
the beginning, he was always the first one to step up and
get to work. He's always in good spirits, too.

As the construction process unfolded, Carlos stood
out as a leader. He's an ambassador for us in the village,
a bridge between Pulse and Libertad. If relationships get
even slightly rocky, he will communicate with us what the
village is saying. That way we find out what they need and
we can adjust our operations accordingly to maintain the
relationship. Carlos naturally progressed into becoming a
manager; we can rely on him to handle maintenance and
work with local staff. We know he's taking care of things.

The village feels the same way about our relationship.

Carlos's whole family lives there; his parents are respected elders, so they know he has their best interests at heart as well. He understands how important it is not to create any tensions or negative relationships; at the same time, he always stands up for what he believes is right.

Carlos treats our center like it's his own. I had an ayahuasca vision about him one night that made me realize I wanted to take care of this guy, his four kids, and his family. When we registered the business, I gave him a percentage. I told him I loved him like a brother and he didn't have to worry about the future.

RETREAT RAISING

Initially, progress on our new facility was swift and smooth. It took only a few selected people a week to clear out all of the overgrowth on the property. The land is close to the riverbank, so we didn't have a lot of overgrown vegetation to cut down, just a few small, bushy trees and tall grass. The villagers did all of the work with machetes and chainsaws.

Time was short, so we needed everything to run on a tight timetable. Unfortunately, securing the wood we needed for construction turned out to be a problem. We had an agreement with the village to send some guys out to harvest wood, which we needed delivered by a certain day. We paid them a percentage of the price we agreed upon and assumed they would make good on their promise. When the first day of building arrived, though, we discovered that only a small portion of the wood was actually delivered.

We had only two months to build a functional retreat center, so this was a huge roadblock for us. I meditated on the situation, trying to decide whether we were going to cancel everything or just try to push it through. We talked with the villagers, explaining our disappointment, the importance of fulfilling their agreement, and the opportunity they had to create a positive ongoing relationship with us. I think they felt a little bit guilty for dragging their heels.

In the end, we decided to go all in. After all, I was already marketing the first retreat with a YouTube series documenting the build. We were selling spots; people were already booked for September. We needed a place for people to stay.

We dug into what we had on-site, tarring wood to protect it from rot, ants, and termites. More wood started rolling in as we worked. By July 31, we were ready to break ground and start building in earnest. About thirty guys, plus our engineer, worked on the construction, starting with the maloca and necessary facilities like toilets and showers. We also began building our two-story riverfront *casa*, though all we had at first was just a platform and a roof.

For a while, we would still depend on the Libertad Jungle Lodge for rooms and meals; guests could stay in the Libertad lodge and come over to us for ceremonies. We also offered a budget option for folks who wanted to tent on the open casa platform. Two or three adventurous guys took us up on that, although they ended up getting soaked when a storm surged in. The rain and wind just tore the tents apart, so those guests ended up in the jungle lodge as well.

HERE AND THERE

The reason that travel is so important to my work is exactly the kind of cultural immersion that made building Pulse Tours and Ayahuasca Adventure Center possible. For me, much of this journey was about stepping outside of the assumptions of my own culture.

CULTURE IS YOUR ENEMY

My thinking about culture has been influenced by writers like Terence McKenna, who actually gave a speech entitled "Culture Is Your Enemy." What I think he meant is that people often don't know how much they have developed based on the influence of their cultural programming. We are all indoctrinated into a culture starting at birth, even if we don't recognize it.

But what is culture? Culture is difficult to define. E. B. Tylor wrote that culture is that complex whole, which includes knowledge, belief, art, morals, law, custom, and any other capabilities and habits acquired by man as a member of society. Culture could also be defined as a social domain that emphasizes the practices, discourses, and material expressions, which over time express the continuities and discontinuities of social meaning of a life held in common.

These definitions have their uses, but for me, culture is simply everything that's human. Language, thought, and belief are all constructs of our culture. Essentially, every aspect of human-related life that touches you on a daily basis is culture.

Recognizing that growing up in one particular culture necessarily shuts you off from other ways of seeing was a transformative moment for me. We all have blind spots, events, and activities we don't question because we were born into them. Likewise, we all have ideas about how our own culture is preferable to others. It's a natural human tendency that leads us to divide ourselves by religion, race, and class. The culture that brought you up naturally forms your perspective.

Travel is one way to step out of your native cultural indoctrination. If you go to Canada and then the United States, you'll have different experiences. Same thing for comparing Texas and California, or China and Japan, or Japan and England. Seeing those differences can help pop the cultural bubble you're standing in. From inside the bubble, everything out there looks weird, scary, incomprehensible, or just plain wrong. When you step outside the bubble, though, you discover that there are so many ways to live that none of them can be the only "right" way, and all of them can teach you something.

One simple example comes from my Canadian upbringing: how a culture handles alcohol. In Canada, drinking alcohol is illegal until you reach a certain age, which only serves to make it that much more attractive to teenagers. People grow up thinking it's cool to get alcohol, so they tend to take it to excess. In Brazil, I was amazed at the open atmosphere around alcohol. It was simply no big deal to buy a beer and walk down the beach with it.

Religion supplies another example. If you grow up in Texas in an evangelical Christian community, it's likely that this particular form of religion is part of life for everyone you interact with. It's taboo to question that, so you don't. It doesn't even occur to you. But if you go to Japan or Thailand and see that there are a lot of very different religious beliefs out there, with a whole different set of rules, you can see your own religion more clearly and make informed decisions about how to participate.

What's interesting about the work we do is that both ayahuasca and adventure are ways to break down barriers like this. People who are drawn to Pulse Tours and Ayahuasca Adventure Center are often seeking that kind of disruption. We get a lot of people at a developmental stage in life—regardless of age—where they're working on which cultural aspects they want to integrate into their developed selves. Ayahuasca and travel are both ways to step outside your usual frame of reference.

Ayahuasca takes that even further. Instead of just stepping outside one area of human culture into another area of human culture, you're stepping outside culture altogether. Psychedelic experiences can give you a depth of awareness that allows you to look at human culture as a whole, with an objective and even critical viewpoint. Ayahuasca ceremonies regularly move me to see the world and how humans interact with the world from an analytical, impartial perspective. All of the distractions of daily life are swept away so I can see it more clearly.

Those distractions are part of our culture, of course. One thing I've noticed from traveling the world is the way Western societies take distraction to an extreme level. The crap that is played on television and just blasted into our field of awareness by increasingly invasive sources creates social conditioning. The distractions are shoved down our throats, training us to become consumers whose problems can only be cured by buying more stuff.

When you're taking ayahuasca, you see through this conditioning. That's why it's such a powerful, transformational medicine. That's why people like Guy Crittenden, whose story we heard earlier, come away from their experience with a new mission—in his case, educating people about what's going on in the world and doing his best to inspire change. It's why Michael Sanders started LOVEolution. (See Michael's story below.)

CULTURE IS YOUR FRIEND

Stepping out of your cultural comfort zone teaches you about yourself relative to your native society. However, to succeed in other communities, you need to understand them, too. Integration is seldom instantaneous, but if you learn how societies work, your learning curve can be a lot shorter.

One framework I found useful working in Peru comes from Geert Hofstede, who described the effects of a society's culture on the values of its members and how these values relate to behavior. Hofstede conducted a worldwide study of employee values in IBM from 1967 to 1973. Hofstede looked at more than seventy countries, extracting data from the forty largest. He later extended his analysis to fifty countries and three regions. His work led him to distinguish between two cultural dimensions (among others) in society: individualism and collectivism. Each person has a place on these scales, but so do nations, regions, and communities, generally speaking. The United States is extremely individualistic, orienting toward personal achievement, appearance, and uniqueness. Stand out in America and you are a success. Japan, by contrast, lives by collectivism, a preference for homogenization. Stand out in Japan and you will be put back in your place with the others.

Understanding these cultural dimensions was very helpful to me in Peru. I could recognize that Libertad had a collectivist culture, where community takes precedence over the individual. Everybody is expected to work together to benefit the larger group. When we negotiate with people in the village like Carlos, we know that he will not do something to benefit himself if it doesn't also benefit the village. If he did, he would be stigmatized, shunned by his people.

It's really refreshing to work with people this way. In modern Western culture, people are expected to just look out for themselves and their immediate families. Striving for individual achievement, status, and wealth often comes at the cost of the community. It may have been different in the past—for instance, in my grandfather's time. He came from humble agricultural roots, where townspeople worked together and money wasn't so integral to life. He was a cheesemaker, someone else was the corn producer, and another person raised cattle. They all came together to create a thriving community. I see the same sort of cooperation in Libertad.

Hofstede wrote about other distinctions that can be made among cultures, such as long-term versus short-term orientation, indulgence versus restraint, task versus personal orientation, and masculinity versus femininity. His writings are valuable to anyone in business and anyone who is interested in learning about culture, travel, and ways to become more immersed in other cultures. His groundbreaking book, *Culture's Consequences: Comparing Values, Behaviors, Institutions and Organizations across Nations*, is a must-read.

MARKETING MICROCULTURES

My master's thesis involved pulling together these ideas

about culture and applying them to a very specific space: successful global adventures companies. I wanted to analyze how these organizations worked and whom they appealed to. Both the business and its customers represented microcultures that I wanted to understand.

I took G Adventures, and specifically their website, as my subject of study. I analyzed how they presented their message and how they described adventure tourism right down to the words, design, and images they incorporated.

The cohesion of the images presented was striking. All of the scenes on the website featured sunny weather, regardless of the season. Even if there was snow on the ground, there was a blue sky above. Populating those scenes were happy people—everybody was smiling—who were almost 100-percent Caucasian. The majority of them were women.

So now I knew what community G Adventures was marketing themselves to, what those people responded to, and how the customer base perceived itself. This was the largest and most successful adventure travel company in the world, in business for more than twenty years, so I felt confident that they knew what they were doing.

Now I also knew how they were doing it, at least from a marketing perspective. I looked at color branding, fonts, design elements, and text. From there, it was a matter of applying similar themes to the Pulse website, which I did. It still serves us well today.

STORIES OF PERSONAL TRANSFORMATION:
MICHAEL SANDERS

Michael Sanders is a partner in Canadian clean energy start-up SunMoon Energy, a partner in LOVEolution: The Evolution of Love on the Dance Floor, and author of *Ayahuasca: An Executive's Enlightenment*. Here, he shares how his ayahuasca experiences have influenced him in business and in life.

"It was around the start of 2013 and I was going through some really dark fatigue. I had no energy, no zest for life, no libido. I had zero sexual drive, and at the time I was only twenty-six years old, so that's a pretty scary experience. I was working as the vice-president of an advertising agency. I was the cofounder of a start-up in the gaming industry, and I was working out and training athletically and intensely about fourteen times per week.

"I was, I think, extremely goal oriented, always go, go, go, never really appreciating what was already happening. I was lacking balance. I was never meditating or doing yoga or anything of that nature. It was always just superintense. I lost my zest for life and was really just going through the motions. I would go into my advertising agency at about noon because I needed so much sleep. I would sleep ten to twelve hours each night and wake up to my alarm clock feeling not a slight bit rested.

"The only thing that would give me any energy would be going to the gym again. I have this love for movement, whether it's parkour or acrobatic dance, or gymnastics, but at that time in my life, my love for it had transformed into an obsession and borderline addiction because it was really the only thing that was making me feel good.

"I consulted with a naturopath, and he had me develop a daily meditation practice and to start focusing on play. Based on his knowledge of my love for movement, he suggested I become far less regimented in my approach and to instead do things that maybe I didn't typically do. Rather than weight lifting and working on gymnastics and all the strength-oriented stuff, to just try rock climbing, where there isn't necessarily a set protocol, or to dance more and to just really play every day and to not treat everything with such intensity.

"I did that, and actually, over the course of four or five months by meditating every day and expressing gratitude every day and playing every day, I started to feel like myself again. It happened faster than I ever expected. Prior to this, I had resolved that if I couldn't figure out how to feel like myself again within the span of two years, that I was going to put a bullet in my brain, because the way I was feeling just wasn't worth continuing at that point in my life.

"Then, in September 2013, one of my best friends, Sid, asked me, 'What are you doing for New Year's this year?'

I didn't know. He said, 'My friend Dan, Dan Cleland, has been running these expeditions throughout South America, and he has been focused on the Amazonian tradition of ayahuasca.'

"Immediately, without Sid giving me any more details, I'm like, 'Man, I'm 100-percent in.' I had heard of ayahuasca through a Joe Rogan podcast interview with Aubrey Marcus. When I first heard about it, I knew at some point I was going to venture down to the jungle and try this strange psychedelic brew, but I just wasn't sure when it would happen. Then here Sid was presenting me with the opportunity.

"I initially thought that ayahuasca would be a recreational experience and then as I started researching and looking more into the diets, I started to understand that this was more like a rite of passage of sorts and that the shamans and the local people in Peru treated it with a great deal of respect. It was a serious endeavor and not something to take lightly.

"I started practicing an ayahuasca diet, which involved no alcohol, no sex, no drugs, no orgasm, no salt, and no spices. Essentially I was just eating white fish, chicken, and some fruits and vegetables. I arrived down in Iquitos on Boxing Day 2013 and was greeted by Dan and Tatyana, who took us around Iquitos for a couple days before we ventured out into the Amazon jungle. That in and of itself was a deeply grounding and profound experience, to just be immersed in this rain forest. It seems so vast that it's infinite. Seeing pink dolphins swimming in the Amazon River, snakes, tarantulas, and lethal animals that our guide, Ricardo, was picking up was a really amazing experience. We were boating in the middle of the night during torrential rain-forest downpours. It was a magical endeavor.

"On New Year's Eve 2013 going into 2014, I was about to have my first ayahuasca ceremony. When I woke up that morning, I meditated and I was feeling more grounded in peace than I had ever had in my entire life. I understood that I was really about to journey into something profound that I didn't necessarily have much real understanding of.

"The shamans in Peru, they speak of mother ayahuasca, this intelligent female entity. They were speaking of ayahuasca as this truly intelligent being and I understood it all as metaphor initially because I couldn't necessarily wrap my head around it as reality.

"I grew up with a father who was a specialist in internal medicine, so I was in a fairly scientific household, not one that was closed-minded by any means, but the notion of communicating with a plant wasn't really part of our worldview. Even the diet—and I've researched nutrition extensively over my life—didn't really make any sense to me, but I was also thinking that if I was going to venture all the way down to Peru, I was going to practice their customs because they probably had their reasons for them.

"On New Year's Eve, we had this flower bath to open

ourselves up to ayahuasca's energy and to protect us from dark energy. Again, that seemed like a metaphor to me, but I was like, 'OK, it's cool. I'll try it.' Then that night, we did a yin yoga, which was this very relaxed yoga practice, where we held postures for three minutes each to invite ayahuasca into our space.

"Toward the end of that yin yoga, rain, thunder, and lightning started pouring through the rain forest. It seemed like an incredible, monumental moment. Then, at eight o'clock in the evening, the ceremony inside the maloca started. The maloca is a beautiful wooden structure that's like a miniature dome, about forty-five-feet tall in the center, with all this intricate woodworking on the inside and screens for windows. There were about twenty-four mattresses in a circle where all of the participants would lie down.

"During our ceremony, I think there were eight guests, including Dan and Tatyana, and then three shamans and two facilitators. I went into my ceremony with two intentions, the first of which was to gain some clarity on my career path. My second intention was to alleviate some of the physical discomfort that I was experiencing in my left upper back that I had attributed to past athletic injuries. I went into the ceremony and among everyone there, I just so happened to be the first to drink the ayahuasca. The shaman invited me up, I sat down, and he poured this earthy, brown liquid. Then he whispered something to the ayahuasca, the brew, and handed it to me, and I whispered my intentions to the ayahuasca.

"I decided to meditate and reflect chronologically on my year because it had been such a teaching year for me. I got to about the month of October in my meditation and I felt this fire shoot up my right arm and start to spread across my torso. I said, 'Mother ayahuasca, can you please give me five more minutes as I finish my reflection on my year? I think it's important that I do so.' I heard this voice respond, 'Yes, my child. Take your time and let me know when you're ready.' Then the fire receded down my arm. At that point, I thrashed my head to the right and then to the left, looking for who the hell said that to me. I realized, 'Holy shit, I'm talking with a plant right now.'

"When I was ready, the fire came back, filled my right arm, and spread across my torso into my legs. I felt this deep and powerful maternal warmth. At that point, purple and green beams of light that looked like the Northern Lights emerged from the darkness. To test their objectivity, I shifted my gaze over to the left and I closed my eyes for a while. Forty-five seconds later, I looked back to where the Northern Lights had been and they weren't there. They had progressed toward me. They were operating like a cloud floats through the sky. It didn't matter whether or not I was looking at them; they were going to continue on their path.

"Then the purple and green beams of light wrapped

themselves around me and turned me over onto my left side into the fetal position. No discredit to my own biological mother, but this was the greatest mother I had ever encountered and I truly understood why the people of Peru refer to her as mother ayahuasca.

"I was lying there in the fetal position thinking, *If this is all the experience is, I'm totally cool with that and I think I'm about ready to fall asleep right now*, because I just felt so at peace. I was about to close my eyes and then, at that moment, the shaman starts singing. They sing these songs called icaros, which they say are not of their own creation, but rather, they channel them through the ayahuasca and through other dimensions.

"He started singing, 'Sowa sowa-wa-wa,' and orange and blue shapes emanated from his mouth and expanded to fill my perceptual field. I was looking at these shapes dancing to the rhythm of his song just wide-eyed with disbelief, and then another shaman started singing his icaros and out of his mouth came these purple and green shapes. The shapes combined while the songs combined in the audio space, creating what seemed to be this visual and auditory symphony.

"Then the only female shaman started singing and a full spectrum of colors exploded from her mouth. [There were] more colors than I'd ever seen before and more colors than there are in the rainbow. All the while, I was hearing the ayahuasca telepathically impart to me,

'Michael, this is a dimension that exists at all times. It's always around you, but you just haven't been consciously aware of it up until this point.'

"I felt the purple and green beams of light wrap around me and elevate me up into this new dimension. Then I felt them sever behind me as an umbilical cord would. I heard ayahuasca say to me, 'Don't worry, my child. There's nothing to fear. Go and explore. I'm here if you need me.' It was the mark of the most wonderful and loving mother, supportive but not suffocating by any means.

"The ayahuasca continued to deliver me to other dimensions where I communicated with spirits that showed me all these different forms of love. The communication was direct. Imagine you were trying to describe the feeling of falling in love to your best friend. If your best friend hasn't experienced the feeling of falling in love, they can intelligibly get a sense of what you're talking about, but unless they've actually had that experience, they can't feel the falling in love.

"Now, rather than using words, imagine you could take your experience of falling in love and place it right inside of him or her. Now your friend understands that experience wholeheartedly. That's what all the communication in this realm is like.

"I ended up having three ceremonies over the course of four days and experienced many different realms and received more lessons than I can count. A lot of that is covered in my book.

"One that stands out, though, [provided] the answers I received to my questions about my career path. I knew that there was something else I needed, aside from my advertising career. It was cool and fun and financially rewarding and I worked with absolutely wonderful people, both in my agency and clients, but I just knew there was something more that I was longing for, my soul was.

"[In response to my questions about my career], the ayahuasca showed me this white porcelain man in chains punching his arms up and ascending through this thick swamp. As he floated upward, he unshackled all of these chains and just let them fall off him. Then he punched his arms up and out to the side and ascended through another version of the same swamp. Then he punched his arms up and out to the side and he kept ascending and ascending. He did this ten times through ten swamps, each time shedding and unshackling more and more chains. I was hearing the name of my start-up, which at the time was called I Wager That. It was just like, 'Just let it go. Let it go. It's not for you. It's a great idea. It's going to be awesome, but your heart's not in it.'

"I said, 'OK, I understand I'm not going to continue on this with this start-up, so what should I do?' She [the ayahuasca] said to me, 'Michael, you've always been a storyteller and you've always wanted to write a book, so write a book.'

"I was like, 'OK, well, if I knew how to make a living out of writing and everything, I'd already be doing that.' She said to me, 'Don't worry about that aspect of it. You're financially secure for now. Just start writing and good things will happen.' Then in this sort of cosmic wink, she said to me, 'I'm giving you a lot to write about.' I laughed. I'm like, 'Yeah, you certainly are.'

"When I came back from Peru, I decided to walk away from the start-up I was working on, and I actually drastically reduced the amount of time I was putting into my ad agency. I reduced it down to four to six hours per week for a while, and I was really focused on writing my book, *Ayahuasca: An Executive's Enlightenment*, and then just really staying open to the possibility of what could come next. I felt this incredibly profound sense of peace that there wasn't necessarily anything I had to do, that I was already complete. From that space is where I can create true magic, to try to make a positive impact, and to just act lovingly and kindly and compassionately and to try to make the world a better place in whatever capacity that is.

"I was focused on the writing, and then there was a period in May 2014 when I was seeing the sun and the moon out every single day for three weeks. I made note of it in my phone because I was like, 'I don't even know if this is astronomically possible, but this is what I'm seeing every day.' Then my former business partner called me and was like, 'Hey, Mike, I want to introduce you to this clean energy start-up that is looking to raise money and I think it's something you'll really resonate with.' The name of the company was Sun Moon Energy.

"I had been learning through the ayahuasca experiences about the interconnectivity of all things and how for any given moment to manifest, all of time and space had to align and conspire for the two of us to meet at this exact point. Then seeing that this company was called SunMoon Energy, I'm like, 'OK, I think the universe is giving me a sign here.' There's this beautiful storyteller that's giving you all these clues if you're open enough to listen to them.

"For the last two years, SunMoon has been on a journey of bringing better energy technologies to market. We're always making progress. It's simply a matter of time before we're starting to distribute them to the world and evolving the way that humans think about and consume energy, so that we can both heal our planet and provide the opportunity for our species to live on Mother Earth for a longer time.

"Meanwhile, I wrote the book, *Ayahuasca: An Executive's Enlightenment*, which was a deeply fulfilling experience for me and so many of the people who have read it. It became an Amazon best seller. One of the things that's most rewarding and humbling for me is all of the people I've had reach out to me and share, pour themselves out to me about their stories and whatever it is that they're going through and every single time I'm initially surprised because I'm like, 'Whoa, I've never even met this person and they're pouring their heart out to me.'

"Then I realize that they feel as though they already know me because I poured myself out to them in my book and I didn't know they were reading it. That's a really cool feeling. Then also, through this new way of being and feeling, this infinite amount of love flowing through the universe and through my own vessel, I was drawn to a group of people to form this musical movement called LOVEolution, which is the evolution of love on the dance floor. We combine shamanic sound therapy with the world's grooviest dance music to infuse humanity and the universe with love. We've hosted eleven celebrations over the past year and they've been the most transcendent, transformative, and uplifting celebrations for everyone who comes. It's the highest vibrational and loving environment and our mission is all about allowing people to be themselves. Our principles are radical inclusion and radical self-expression. We provide a space where people don't have to worry about what it is that they're trying to be or societal notions of what is cool or what is right. You can just come here and everybody's welcome and we accept you and it's a place of unconditional love. We've hosted eleven celebrations throughout the greater Toronto area over the past year, and now we're doing a couple in Los Angeles and we're hosting a camp at Burning Man this year. It has been a fairy-tale ride of love and wonder and magic, being able to create these experiences and liberating people from any limitations that they've imposed on themselves.

"My time at Pulse Tours and Ayahuasca Adventure Center set me on this path, and specifically Dan and Tatyana. They're just two of the most absolutely loving and wonderful people I've encountered and they feel like a brother and sister to me. I think it's really wonderful everything that they're doing because I know they've helped an astounding number of people.

"I haven't felt called to drink ayahuasca since my time in the jungle and I actually don't have any intentions of doing so. It's not to say that I never will drink it again. I feel as though I've learned a lot from it and I know there's still an infinite world to explore with it."

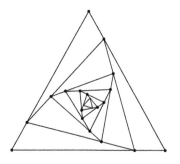

CHAPTER FIVE

BUMPS IN THE ROAD

TODAY, I CAN LOOK AROUND AND SEE THE BEAUTI-
ful center we built and greet the people who come to
experience it. However, during the initial development,
it sometimes felt like we were taking one step forward
and two steps back.

GROWING PAINS

A PLACE TO STAY

Financially, we walked a bit of a tightrope at first. We had
money from my parents, but it wasn't enough to finish
building the center. To keep the momentum going, we had
to book passengers for spaces that didn't yet physically
exist. We took reservations with a 50-percent deposit and
used that money to fund the next leg of construction. We

were so determined. Even though financing the project this way essentially meant borrowing from our customers for about six months—a big risk—we felt it was worth doing because we were building something that would ultimately serve our guests well and pay for itself several times over.

To keep costs down, we initially intended to build on a fairly small scale. We planned on a maloca, toilets, showers, and the riverfront casa, which would house the gym, an office, a lounge, and my bedroom. The Libertad Jungle Lodge was close by, cheap, and convenient, so we thought we would continue to rent lodging space there.

At first, this arrangement seemed pretty solid. Manuel, the owner of the lodge, worked well with us for a few months, but by October, he was booking our reserved spaces out to other guests and springing the news on us at the last minute. I was in a panic. People had paid good money to come to our program, and we had reserved space for them six months in advance, but now Manuel was telling me there was no place for them to stay. I eventually convinced him to make space for us for that session, but he pulled the same trick again a month or so later.

By this time, I was yelling, pleading, and offering to pay double. I explained how much business we would bring to his lodge, but Manuel wouldn't budge. The person who booked his guests through Trip Advisor didn't coordinate those reservations with ours at all, and Manuel wasn't willing to risk his online reputation by changing his Trip Advisor bookings. So, it was our reputation that was set up to take the hit.

With less than two days' notice before the retreat was to start, I had to go out and buy beds, blankets, mosquito nets, and pillows and fill the riverfront casa with beds. It looked like a two-story dormitory, girls in one spot and guys in another. We still needed a kitchen, but we at least had sleeping quarters, a ceremonial space, and restrooms, so technically, we were in business for the next group.

Manuel did end up letting us use his kitchen; I think he felt a little bit bad for how things had gone. For the next couple of trips, we continued buying our own food and paying Manuel's staff to cook it, but we needed our own kitchen. It was a good thing we rushed to complete it, because before long, Manuel kicked us out of his kitchen as well. We were bringing in high-quality food that made the scant fare Manuel provided for his guests look unappetizing. Our group would sit there, happily eating beautiful fruits and delicious meals, while his people stared at us, wondering where their meals were. His reputation was suffering by comparison, so he wanted us to disappear.

For a few weeks, we compromised. I bought tables and chairs for the casa and Manuel had his people bring food over to our place. By November, though, our kitchen was ready, so we had all of the facilities necessary to host retreats. We didn't stop there, though. The dormitories were getting crowded, so we started working on guest rooms right away. We had a couple of guest rooms completed by New Year's, plus a room for the shamans, a room Tatyana and I shared, and a hammock lounge. We eventually added four guest rooms with three-person occupancy.

The roadblocks seemed endless, but I didn't spend a lot of time wallowing in worry. One of the valuable skills I developed while leading G Adventures tours was maintaining calm in the face of drama. When you're trying to get fifteen people from Bahia to São Luís, Brazil, you can't find a bus, and someone in the group suffers a diabetic stroke, you learn to adjust very quickly.

The ability to think on my feet came in very handy during the frantic building process. The schedule was so tight that the first guests were expected on the same day we were supposed to finish the plumbing and water systems. We couldn't waste a minute, so if we needed anything, I would make the trek to Iquitos—two hours on the road and two hours on a boat—to retrieve supplies.

There were only three of us—Tatyana, Ricardo, and I—handling most of the guest-related work, everything from buying groceries to facilitating ceremonies to leading jungle trips. Add to this mediating the inevitable personality clashes that would crop up in each group of guests. We were all exhausted.

One day when we had a day off between ceremonies, Tatyana and I stayed in a hotel for a night. I remember closing the door, falling back against the wall, and sliding to the floor. I was frayed. I had nothing left to give.

A night of semiluxury refreshed us, however, in time for the next day's ceremony. Our first groups were generally amiable; one participant took a midretreat break, but he came back to finish. In fact, he has been back several times since. Our previous experience managing group dynamics helped us negotiate situations like this.

RESPONSES AND RESPONSIBILITIES

The thing about serving people is that you never know how they will behave or what will happen. One night after a ceremony, for instance, we cut up some pineapple to share with everyone. It didn't seem like a recipe for disaster. Unfortunately, one of the guests, unbeknown to us, was hypoglycemic. While everyone else was praising the delicious gift from God they were enjoying, this man collapsed in the hallway. He recovered quickly on his own—he'd had a blood sugar spike from the pineapple—but it shook him up. In the end, his experience taught him, and us, a lot. We all learned a lesson about how precious life is.

Problems didn't always come from the outside, of course. There were also rifts in our small community, some of them painful, like the break with our close friend, Ricardo. Without his help, we never could have built the Ayahuasca Adventure Center. We depended on him. But one night, after we had been working together for a year and a half, I overheard some young women talking about his conduct in a way that concerned me. He was clearly overstepping his boundaries with them. We don't have a lot of rigid rules at Pulse, but the number one, unbreakable rule is that all of us, especially those in positions of power, demonstrate unwavering respect for the women in our groups.

I was furious. I couldn't sleep that whole night. There was still so much adrenaline pumping through my veins even in the morning that it was difficult to talk to Ricardo. I told him what I had heard; right away, he knew exactly what I was talking about. He tried to blame it on the ladies. That was the last straw for me; we threw him off the property. He has never been back.

We have since made a public commitment to zero tolerance to any kind of sexual harassment or inappropriate touching. We are close to our staff, but we still need to maintain vigilance. When a similar incident occurred several years ago, we immediately severed ties with the employee in question. At our center or anywhere else, it's imperative that management knows what is going on in the day-to-day operations so situations like this don't arise.

SEEKING A SHAMAN

Also key to the whole enterprise was choosing the right shaman. We met our lead shaman, Wiler, in 2012, and got to know him during the 2013 June Solstice retreat. Unlike many shamans, who keep themselves separate from the community, Wiler was out walking around and talking to people every day. He was always curious, asked a lot of questions, and generally chatted folks up. I noticed him for that and also for his unique appearance: Wiler has one brown eye and one blue—and blind—eye as a result of a fishing accident when he was a young man.

Over the next year, I watched how Wiler worked and was always impressed. I was so interested in working with him that I made a scouting expedition to his village to see if it was a place I would feel comfortable bringing guests. The place was just too rustic, with no facilities at all, so we decided against it. As fate would have it, though, Wiler had stopped working at the center where we met him, so he was out of work at exactly the moment I was looking for a shaman for our soon-to-be center.

One of the reasons the other center let Wiler go, ironically, was one of the reasons I wanted him to come work with us. Wiler has a mesmerizing deep voice that brings power to his ceremonies. He put this gift to good use when the lead shaman at his center was unable to run ceremonies. Wiler took over and he was a rock star in there. He was too good to continue working under someone else. I have always wondered if maybe he lost his position because the other shaman felt a bit threatened by the apparent competition for lead voice.

It was important to me to bring on a shaman I knew

and respected. You can't just go shopping for shamans. Well, you can, but the chance of getting someone skilled, dependable, honest, and trustworthy is very slim. We got very lucky with Wiler. He is still with us and we hope he will stay for a long time to come. We rely on him to make the medicine, lead ceremonies, and choose additional shamans to work on our team.

COMING HOME

Putting together the ayahuasca retreat center took nearly two years. Of course we never really stop working on it, although we are well settled now. There are still upgrades to make—solar power, satellite Internet access, and so forth—but we have a strong, comfortable home base.

The last year actually saw us add a couple of new buildings higher up on the property to provide a safe haven in case of floods. We originally built slightly above the normal water line, but in 2015, we got what was referred to as a "hundred-year flood." We actually had one of our biggest groups ever booked that March and we were forced out of the center by the flooding. Luckily, we found a nice lodge called Yacumama just up the Yarapa River that let us use their facilities, although it did mean hauling twenty mattresses over there to set up a ceremonial space.

The water kept on coming, however, and soon we were flooded out of Yacumama. By this time, at least 80 percent of the lodges in the area submerged. There was water everywhere. We headed to higher land in a town called Tamshiyacu. The lodge wasn't actually ready for us, but we paid them up front so they could upgrade their toilet facilities and such before we arrived for a three-week stay.

The Tamshiyacu lodge was not the perfect solution. We had a large group with eighteen men and one woman. There were a number of big, burly guys in the group, putting a lot of testosterone in the air. Fights broke out among guests and escalated to battles between competing shamans. One ceremony got quite heated and some of the guests actually stepped up to act as security.

We moved around quite a bit after that, frantically searching for a place that would serve us well. Staff members were getting upset and threatening to leave because it was all so tense and out of control. Finally, we found a beautiful place called the Wild Yarapa Lodge. These guys were awesome. They had a beautifully crafted lodge with private rooms, electricity, and a satellite phone. We moved in there for the final month of the flooding and had an excellent experience. Still, everyone was ready to go back home.

Thanks to our loyal friend Carlos, our home was fine when we returned. Carlos and his family moved in while we were gone—they built a platform in the gym and strung up a couple of hammocks—and took care of the place. We had a big cleaning job ahead of us, because the river moved a lot of debris through our property, but the village people pitched in to scrub the place up. The buildings, made of solid hardwood, were fine, but we did have to clean out some frogs and barnacles from underneath structures.

We were so glad to be back; we didn't ever want to be in the precarious position of begging for a place to stay ever again. Right away, we started new construction a meter and a half higher. We now have a second, smaller maloca, new guest rooms, new toilets and showers, and hammocks up there.

Even if I had known how tough the building would be and all of the challenges we would face in our first year, I would still have launched this project. I love the place. It's awesome, and the amount of enjoyment other people have gotten out of it has been worth all the trouble.

FINDING OUR FOOTING

While working with other shamans and other centers, we learned about a wide variety of practices. There were some elements we loved and would definitely use, but there were others we knew we would have to modify. One of these elements is the preceremony purge. I understood the value of doing a purge to initiate a retreat, but my experiences had not always been positive.

One ceremony in particular stands out because it was the one my father came to and the one that turned him off from trying ayahuasca. We were at a different center, and the purgative they used was extremely difficult to manage. Participants were feeling so bad before the ceremony that they didn't want to go through with it. I knew there had to be a better way.

Our answer was to use kambo, a paste that is applied to the skin, prompting a quick, effective purge. Kambo doesn't require the participant to imbibe anything. Harvesting the kambo medicine involves a nighttime walk in the jungle in search of the so-called monkey frogs that live twenty or thirty feet up in the trees. Kambo harvesters climb the trees and capture several frogs at a time. The frog is not killed; in fact, it isn't harmed at all. Instead, it is tickled on the nose until it starts secreting a toxin from glands on its back. The toxin is gathered, sometimes cured with smoke, and then applied to the skin. To facilitate absorption, a tiny stick is first burned to a glowing red ember and quickly poked into the skin. It doesn't really hurt; it just allows the medicine to absorb faster.

Kambo is made up of nine bioactive peptides that affect the gastrointestinal muscles, gastric and pancreatic secretions, blood circulation, the adrenal cortex, and the pituitary gland. The outward effects include increased heart rate and temperature, sweating, and a rise in blood pressure, along with the urge to vomit. Because kambo works so deep inside your body, it's a very effective purgative.

The whole experience lasts only ten or fifteen minutes.

It's uncomfortable, but it cleans out the body and energizes the person. Our kambo shaman says it is also an immune booster because it activates the body's immune response system. We offer kambo to everyone on day two of every retreat, although participation is always optional.

Johnny Java is our kambo shaman. He comes from the Matses tribe, also known as the Jaguar people, who were great warriors. Our guests get up in the morning, drink some masato or papaya juice, and gather in the maloca where Johnny applies the medicine. If he's not there, Tatyana is also trained to administer the kambo.

We started using kambo back at Manuel's lodge, where our efforts were less than appreciated. It may have been one of the things that caused our split. We didn't have any privacy at this lodge, so we would do our kambo ceremony out in the open. If you don't know what you're seeing, the whole thing can look quite strange, as it involves fire and vomiting. Plus, we end the ceremony by dumping water over the participant's head. It's pretty dramatic. Manuel and his workers didn't understand what we were doing.

The experience was yet another clue that we needed to have our own place to work.

HOW DOES IT FEEL?

Perception is everything, and some people perceive ceremonies like ours as dangerous. It's a myth we work hard to dispel. Certainly, people have had adverse reactions to ayahuasca, but it's very rare. An extremely small percentage of folks have an allergic reaction, but that's true of any substance.

Frequently, during ceremonies, one or two people have dramatic responses to the medicine, but that is just part of the process. They might feel frightened and move around the maloca, vocalizing their experience, for instance. Our facilitators are always there to help people through the encounter, though. This focused support is one of the elements of our retreats that participants appreciate most. We not only give them the space to release all of their pent-up energy and the psychological demons they're wrestling with, but we also provide plenty of personal support.

On the opposite end of the spectrum, some people have trouble connecting with the medicine and feel minimal effects. A few people feel something but don't experience visions. It's disappointing, but repeated attempts usually complete the connection.

Safety within the ceremony is extremely important to us, as is the well-being of all of the guests staying at our property. Early on, we had a scare with a missing passenger that led us to put physical safety at the top of our priority list. I was traveling when I got an e-mail from the team with the subject line: URGENT—PASSENGER MISSING. My stomach dropped. That morning, following a ceremony, one of the participants was missing from the group. The ceremony had gone fine and everyone gathered peacefully afterward, but in the morning, one man was gone.

There weren't a lot of great scenarios for what could have happened. Our place is in the middle of the jungle, right by the river. We're not connected to anything by road. Our security team had been in their usual spot in front, along the river, but they hadn't seen anything. We didn't have security out back because the jungle is so thick that it's just impossible to navigate. We thought surely nobody would try.

I hoped that he had just wandered over to Libertad and was someplace safe by now, but it took a while to find him. My staff scoured the property, eventually finding clues at the very edge of the jungle: a towel, a footprint, and a half-eaten apple. A couple more footprints led into the jungle. A handful of staff members followed the trail for hours until it ended, ominously, at the edge of the Yarapa River.

Everyone was frantic by now, but it turned out he was close by, in the village of Puerto Miguel. He had walked barefoot through the jungle all night and wound up in one of the villager's huts. I was so relieved to hear this. My staff took him back to Iquitos, where he recovered quickly. He actually returned to the center to complete his retreat.

We have had some challenging sessions, and I've taken on some unhealthy stress trying to cover all the bases. I think any entrepreneur will say that some days they are sure they've made the right decision, and on other days they just want to hide in a dark room until the latest storm blows over. The stakes get higher as you continue to build your business; when you start out, you don't have much to lose, but once you've built something tangible, the risk feels different.

This was definitely a time of maturation for me. I went from having nobody to worry about except myself to being responsible for a business, property, staff, and guests in a fairly short time. I used to be just a guy on the beach, but now I'm responsible for other people's lives. The first time we made some money, I was sorely tempted to spend it all on immediate gratification, but I had to think about what investments would be best for the business. It was tough at first, but eventually I made the mental transition to realizing I was the decision maker, not the laborer, and it was my job to look at the big picture. That let me control my schedule and stress a lot better.

STORIES OF PERSONAL TRANSFORMATION:
DONALD BUMANGLAG

Donald "Donnie" Bumanglag is a thirty-four-year-old father of four, a veteran combat medic, and a posttraumatic stress disorder (PTSD) survivor. Feeling trapped and suicidal following his three military tours, Donnie found inspiration in a TED Talk about ayahuasca. He made his way to Pulse Tours and Ayahuasca Adventure Center, where he tried the medicine and subsequently turned his life around. Donnie's story has been featured on *Alternet*, *The Drunken Taoist*, and YouTube. Here, he speaks specifically about his transformation through ayahuasca.

"Before ayahuasca, my life was in turmoil. I was a US Army Airborne Ranger who left [the service] highly decorated and after a few shitty jobs went into law enforcement. I spent almost ten years as a cop after being a soldier, and I started having really bad issues with PTSD and traumatic brain injury from my time in Afghanistan and Iraq.

"After three deployments and years of wondering, I sought help through the Department of Veterans Affairs. However, throughout their process, I grew dependent on selective serotonin reuptake inhibitors (SSRIs) and benzodiazepines to quell my ever-growing anxious tendencies. I was sad and overweight. I was in a really dark place. I eventually had to retire from law enforcement after I could no longer maintain any semblance of a sleep schedule.

"Shortly after, I found cannabis and found a counter-culture which included the *Joe Rogan Experience* podcast and eventually [journalist and author] Graham Hancock. After hearing of the medicinal uses of ayahuasca from Hancock's banned TED Talk, I started researching the plant medicine. It took me months to find the courage to make the journey, but my life is significantly better from this short experience. I saw ayahuasca as my last shot and for me, it paid off in a big way. Ayahuasca gave me my life back. My wife has a husband and my kids have a father because of ayahuasca.

"The medicine is undeniable. Ayahuasca taught me more about myself in a few hours than I learned gaining a degree or through years of psychotherapy and pharma guinea-pigging. It is highly personal and provides an experience that is uniquely its own when done in such an indigenous rural setting. Words don't possess the power and love that could possibly show what ayahuasca can do for a guy like me. It was life changing.

"The experience for me is as important as sex, as important as war is in my identity; it is a fundamental part of who I am now. I was freed from a large majority of the hate I had for my past and with shocking ease I was able to restructure those memories for myself.

"It was as though I was able to catalog my memories and shine some light on the worst parts and keep the good parts at the same time. I was amazed at how quickly it becomes clear that we all possess the tools within for what it takes to heal us. In our own prison we are the only holders of the key. Ayahuasca allows a space where the participant can be shown both the purest forms of personal accountability as well as the purest forms of love.

"I was amazed at how effective and how personal the process is. It was as though the drug allowed me to view a picture show of my own life, as though there was an internal camera recording how I affected others not only in my own home but on the other side of the earth. I could quickly see where some of my lines of thinking had become toxic and where the changes needed to occur. Spiritually, ayahuasca took me to a place that challenged me personally as significantly as any elite law enforcement training or military operation.

"Ayahuasca taught me a few things. The first was that honesty and intention [are] what are needed to create true behavioral changes. The second major lesson was that if I wanted to help myself, I had to go back to helping others.

"After leaving the retreat, I've had the urge to share the parts of my story as it relates to war, at least the parts that I am legally allowed to share, because I feel that war no longer benefits the human race, and it's painful to watch kids head off for the same future and life lessons I had to see. Before ayahuasca, I didn't have that level of empathy.

"Many small changes have happened. I quit watching

football and basically stopped supporting companies that don't support their people. I take time to read more and I shut off my cable television. I eat organic food now and I pay attention to the chemicals that go into the food supply of myself and my family. I'm also much more active than before, I spend much more time in nature, and have taken up Brazilian jiu-jitsu with some other veterans in my similar predicament. It's still a struggle at times, but ayahuasca made me see that life was worthwhile, and for that, I'm forever thankful.

"My wife tells people ayahuasca gave her her husband back, and I think she's right."

PART THREE

—

FULL SPEED AHEAD

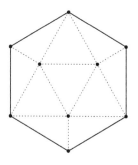

CHAPTER SIX

THE EVOLUTION

FROM THE START, WE WANTED PULSE TOURS AND Ayahuasca Adventure Center to stand out in the crowd. All of my research and study of entrepreneurship confirmed that it was essential to be different in a readily identifiable way. While we haven't necessarily created our own market, we have carved out a particular corner of the ayahuasca space.

The people who come to the center tend to be young, health- and fitness oriented, adventurous, open-minded explorers with a fresh outlook on the world. We get plenty of people who are middle aged or older and not as attached to the physical aspects of our experience, but we have always emphasized the adventure side of the operation.

In January 2015, I decided to add a gym to the center.

For me, personally, it was important to have a way to get regular exercise, and I knew our guests could benefit from that, too. No other ayahuasca center has a true gym. Some places offer yoga classes, but none of them has a fully equipped fitness gym like we do.

We also emphasized our jungle tours right from the start. A few other centers have expanded into jungle excursions as well; that's a direct result of the trend we initiated. We became popular on AyaAdvisors.org for our jungle adventures and then we noticed several other places promoting similar packages. It feels great to be a leader, but it's also important to maintain our own identity.

In the beginning, we got some flak for being different. Because our philosophy includes a healthy dose of fun, we have been called the "spring break" of ayahuasca centers. Ayahuasca is not often spoken of in the same sentence as adventure, even though they are really very compatible. People doing ayahuasca ceremonies are going on spiritual journeys to confront their personal demons. What better way to do it than a pilgrimage across the world, into the middle of the jungle where they test themselves in the face of adversity? It's the same sort of work. One can inform the other, encouraging total integration.

Physical movement can facilitate the processing of mental breakthroughs, which is important after receiving the lessons of ayahuasca. Exercise helps to bring awareness into the body following the psychologically challenging work of the ceremonies. It gives people a bit of a mental break. Also, exercising in the jungle, where it is extremely hot and humid, makes you sweat buckets. This helps complete the cleansing.

Our gym is outfitted with fitness equipment from Onnit, including battle ropes, kettle bells, steel maces, martial arts equipment, and a heavy bag and boxing gloves. We've personalized some of it for our location. The kettle bells are shaped like monkey heads and one of the maces features a cast iron mold of an Alex Grey painting. (Grey is known for his psychedelic and spiritual paintings.)

My relationship with Onnit began in 2014, when I connected with its founder, Aubrey Marcus. We originally talked about doing a supplement program for the center. Further research made Aubrey cautious about combining certain supplements with ayahuasca, so we didn't pursue that. The Onnit-equipped gym, however, has been a big hit. People who know a lot about ayahuasca are familiar with Aubrey Marcus and his business partner Joe Rogan through their podcasts. People often get their first introduction to the medicine from listening to Aubrey's and Joe's stories.

I spent some time in Austin, getting certified on their equipment and meeting Aubrey. I also enjoyed getting to know the rest of the Onnit team and have made some really good friends, have had some really good times, and am now working on side projects with a few of the guys

I met there. Onnit is an example of a lifestyle and way of doing business that I aspire to developing for myself.

Although Aubrey hasn't yet ventured down to the Aya-huasca Adventure Center, I have enjoyed developing a friendship with him and have taken more than a few lessons from his lead. In fact, if it wasn't for Aubrey, I'd still be typing out this manuscript, struggling to finish. He put me in touch with Tucker Max, the founder of Book In A Box. If it wasn't for Book In A Box, you wouldn't be reading this right now. Their team expediently took this book from idea to publication in a matter of about six months in an incredibly professional and refined manner.

During most of our retreats, a number of people use the gym every day. Usually, there are two or three people working out between ceremonies. About 50 percent of our participants spend time in the gym; they love it. All of our staff members exercise there. Having a gym at the "office" is a pretty nice perk, especially when the "office" is an open-air complex that overlooks a five-hundred-meter-wide river and a 2.2 million hectare nature reserve.

While I understand the marketing value of defining our niche as exciting and adventurous, it honestly grew out of our personal interests and passions. We love being immersed in a pristine jungle environment, taking tours to see jungle animals, and keeping our bodies healthy with regular exercise and healthy foods. We simply embraced what we had sought for ourselves so we could bring it to others.

Interestingly, our unique approach actually opens up the ayahuasca experience to people who might not have considered this before. People who are really skeptical of the ideology, or total atheists, are more likely to think about starting their exploration at a place like Pulse, where we don't insist people strictly adhere to a particular ideology. Several participants have told us that they chose our center because our website didn't appear as exotic, or "woo-woo," as some others.

We still follow the traditions of the plant medicine and the shaman's spiritual guidance, but we try to open it up to be more universally acceptable. There's not a lot of jargon to learn, for instance. Where traditional ceremonies use words like *God* and *demons*, we tend to say "Universe" and "negative energies." We want to make the experience more accessible, not less.

HOW IT HAPPENS

By the end of 2014, we had developed five primary programs. We work around a seven-day core into which we integrate four ceremonies, two or three jungle excursions, and plenty of group activities. The shortest option is our seven-day Amazon Ayahuasca Adventure, which includes four ayahuasca ceremonies, a kambo ceremony, and a nunu ceremony (a Matses tribal tobacco ceremony that clears the breath and the mind), plus three days of jungle tours. The fourteen-day Intensive Ayahuasca Retreat allows deeper immersion through eight ayahuasca ceremonies and additional jungle time. People who choose this package often enjoy days spent swimming with the river dolphins. For a twenty-one-day program, which we call the 21-Day Total Human Transformation, folks really go all in, participating in twelve ayahuasca ceremonies, kambo and nunu, and all of the jungle adventure they can handle. Often, during the third week, people spend some of their time exercising in the gym or relaxing in the hammocks.

Beyond the monthly retreats we also offer tours up to Machu Picchu and an annual New Year's celebration. For the Machu Picchu tour, we first meet people in Cusco to take them to experience San Pedro with a healer up in the mountains. Then we explore the Inca ruins. Our guests get a close look at Inca culture, learn about indigenous Q'ero shamanism, and see mountain creatures like the condor. Doing all of this during the day, through the lens of San Pedro, offers a different perspective from the ayahuasca. We really try to offer a multidimensional experience.

Finally, our year ends with a ten-day New Year's package. This celebratory retreat offers a truly unique alternative to the usual New Year's glitz; we trade ballrooms and champagne for a New Year's Eve ceremony and fireworks with the villagers of Libertad. Everybody walks over to the village together at midnight—just after an ayahuasca ceremony—as we transition from one year to the next. The evening is often contemplative; guests meditate on what went right and wrong in the past year and what they would like to change for the future.

Newcomers to ayahuasca often think that they need to do longer retreats to really get the full benefits, but they can go pretty deep in just seven days. Often, people will come for seven days, go back to their lives and integrate some of their lessons, and then return to us for a longer stay. It's like peeling an onion; it takes time to peel all the layers off and get right down to the core. The longer folks stay with us, the deeper they can go, but their choice depends on where they are in their lives.

The growth curve is pretty steep in the beginning; it takes a few ceremonies to break through and clean out all of the blockages that have accumulated and calcified over the years. Then, once you become open, you can come back periodically for a refresher. Refreshers don't need to be so long. The way ayahuasca works for me, personally, is that I need to do only one ceremony every three to six months to keep feeling cleansed. It's like pushing the Reset button.

Of course people also consider practical matters like how much time and money they have to spend on doing a retreat. Honestly, though, what are your choices? You could go on a Mexican vacation for two weeks, blow several thousand dollars getting drunk and sunburned, or you could cleanse your body and refine your mind in Iquitos and go back home with new ideas and a new perspective.

Cost is always a factor. Happily, we have been able to reduce our rates after building our own facilities because we don't have to pay a middleman anymore. We are not the cheapest in the area, but we're not the most expensive either. One thing that drives our fee structure is our commitment to treating our staff well. We want to make sure we are paying them the rate they deserve, which in turn ensures that our guests have the benefit of dedicated, experienced staff. If you are to rank us, price-wise, among ayahuasca centers, we would probably be third or fourth on the list, although we also provide extra services like the jungle tours and gym, so it's difficult to compare.

MULTITASKING MISTAKES

We're dedicated to providing a good work-life balance for all of Pulse's employees; this is a lesson I had to learn personally and, perhaps not surprisingly, the hard way. Once we had developed the business to the point that it was running and thriving, I started looking for other places to put my creative energy. I was the classic "artist" entrepreneur whom Tony Robbins talks about; I needed to create.

My first side project was a yoga and surf retreat in Panama that would integrate some plant medicine healing as well. I got pretty close to signing on a remote property there, but it became clear that the place wasn't just remote; it was nearly inaccessible. I couldn't see handling an emergency from such a location, so I let the deal fall through, even though we had already started promoting it. I couldn't ignore the pit in my stomach that told me this was a bad idea. In business, you need to trust your instincts.

I still wanted a new project, though. It came my way in Austin, Texas, in the form of a kratom company. Kratom is a plant medicine that can restore energy and reduce pain, and I was always interested in ways to maximize the human experience, so it seemed like a good fit. There was a huge customer base in Texas, so that's where I went.

I jumped right into the kratom venture, set up an interim, make-do production facility to package products in a Houston condo, established the corporation and managed bank accounts, and navigated the supply chain, production, and shipping. It was a huge undertaking, and I have to admit that the launch did not happen as quickly as it could have due to my inexperience and lack of available time.

The whole time I was rushing around Houston, and eventually Austin, managing kratom production, I was also involved in Pulse Tours and Ayahuasca Adventure Center in Peru. I had to leave my kratom operation unsupervised every time I went to Peru. It was feasible to manage it all, but only if both businesses were running smoothly. As soon as anything went wrong, the stress levels escalated.

Ultimately, my kratom employees turned out to be extremely unreliable; some even stole from me, their employer. That was the final straw. I realized I had bitten off way more than I could chew. After six or seven months, I decided to sell the business to a customer. It was a successful exit, with a small profit attached, but the biggest thing I took away from this experience was the knowledge that it's not worth starting a business if you can't put 100 percent on the table.

The whole enterprise was likely ego-related. It's a classic novice mistake for entrepreneurs to make: assuming that their success in one area assures success in all areas. You start thinking you've got the golden touch, so you start taking bigger risks, not realizing how big a role luck played all along.

STORIES OF PERSONAL TRANSFORMATION: RANDY M.

Randy M. (not his real name) fought depression every day until he discovered ayahuasca. He suffered severe posttraumatic stress disorder from incidents that occurred during his time in the Coast Guard, and he tried every medical solution offered to him. Not until he found Pulse Tours and Ayahuasca Center did Randy understand what it really meant to be happy. He shares his story here.

"I was depressed my whole life. Since birth, since my earliest memory, I had been depressed. I always felt like I was just different from other people and didn't really understand why other people were happy all the time, how that can be possible. My whole life, growing up, I had some depression going on, but then some things happened when I was in the Coast Guard. I joined the Coast Guard after high school. Also, through high school, there were times where I was depressed and I would take mushrooms, those psychedelic mushrooms, and those would really help me out. They would help me out, but it would be temporary... The depression would come back. Then, of course, when I went to the Coast Guard, I couldn't do that anymore.

"I joined the Coast Guard thinking that I was going to save people's lives and stop cocaine trafficking from coming into the country... I was a boarding team member, so I was doing law enforcement with the Coast Guard. I was on a ship, and we had a small boat that we would put in the water and go do boardings.

"There was one time, we were in between Florida and the Bahamas. We got information that this boat loaded with cocaine was going to come by... We were the only boat that could intercept them. I was nineteen years old, I was really pumped up because I'm about to go on this boarding that could be life or death. I might have to shoot somebody, or might get shot at. Honestly, I didn't want to. But I was nineteen years old; I felt pretty macho. I was kind of brainwashed in the Coast Guard to be this tough guy.

"The boat was supposed to pass us in two hours, so we got ready immediately, and we were ready to go in the water, in the small boat, but the time kept passing. They didn't put us in the water. We were all looking around at one another like, 'What the hell's going on?' Eventually, we saw this boat, and it was off in the distance, and it changed course so that it was coming straight at us. Then, they had these machine guns up on the side of the boat, so I was thinking, *Oh, at any moment they're just going open fire on this boat with the machine guns. It's coming toward us. There are people up there. There are men on the machine guns aimed at this boat.* I thought any second, they were going to start firing on it, but they never did.

"Then, at the last second, this boat came maybe fifty yards away from our ship, and right past us and [they] waved at us. There [were] big bales of what I'm assuming was cocaine. I'm thinking, *What the hell just happened?* Even our captain told us, "That's not the boat we're looking for," even though we saw it with our own eyes. It fit the description and everything, a long, thin boat with big outboard motors, and it's going fast, hauling ass carrying drugs to the United States, and it was obvious that that was the one, but our captain told us, "That's not the one," and then told us to do a boarding on this other boat that had two men on it who were just fishing. Literally, they were just out fishing. We arrested them, and took them back to the boat.

"From this point forward, I have nothing to do with it. I had a feeling that I knew what was about to happen. They tied the guys up in the back and beat the shit out of them, tortured them. They were on the back of the boat for like a day and a half, being beaten constantly. They were trying to get a confession from these innocent fishermen, saying that they were drug traffickers, so we can say that we caught the bad guys. I put two and two together and realized that—or assumed, I should say—that this boat that was carrying cocaine had paid someone off. I told them I'd rather be dead than to take part in this.

"That's when I really shut down and became more depressed than ever before in my life. At this point, they have us brainwashed that if you deny orders to that extent, they'll kill you, or they'll throw you in prison forever, but

I didn't care. Those options were just fine for me. I would rather be killed or put in prison forever than frame innocent people and let drug traffickers go.

"Then, the medic on the boat pulled me aside, and he was one of my only friends on the boat, and he didn't agree with what was happening on the boat, so he told me he knew a way out. If I cooperated with him, then I could get out of the Coast Guard and have an honorable discharge. I said, 'OK, sure. I'll do anything. I'll play the game; just tell me what to do.' He said that I have to say that I'm suicidal, that I want to kill myself, and then they have to put me on antidepressants. Then, once I'm on antidepressants, then I will have to be processed out of the Coast Guard, but I'll get an honorable discharge. I just have to not talk about what happened. I said, 'Fine, that's the deal. I'll do it. I'll play the game. I'll act like I want to kill myself.'

"In my mind, I was thinking, as soon as I get out of the Coast Guard, I'm just going to stop taking these antidepressants. They didn't tell me that you can't do that. They didn't tell me that these drugs, you have to taper yourself off because there are really severe withdrawals and side effects. They put me on Paxil. They put me on the maximum dose of Paxil to start with.

"[Paxil has] been sued for over a billion dollars by families of people who take it and then kill themselves. They miss a dose, or they try and quit, and they kill themselves because they just have to go through the withdrawals, or begin them, and flip out and kill themselves. They can't handle it. I didn't know that. I got out of the Coast Guard. Nobody told me that, so I got out of the Coast Guard, I'm processed out of the Coast Guard. I'm on cloud nine. I'm just happy to get out, so I stopped taking the pills. I just threw them away.

"I was living at my mom's house, and then within twenty-four or forty-eight hours, the withdrawals started, and then this began a really dark part of my life. For the first time in my life, I honestly wanted to kill myself. I had a gun in my closet. I had somehow, whenever this withdrawal started, somehow, some part of me told me to hide the bullets from myself. I was so out of it that I couldn't remember where the bullets were. I had the gun in my hands, and I'm looking for the bullets, looking for the bullets, frantically looking for the bullets in my closet. As soon as I found them, I was just going to load the gun and just shoot myself in the head, just be done with everything. I got frantic.

"I was at my mom's house, and it just flashed in my head, like, 'What happens to my mom if she hears a gunshot and comes in and sees her son just shot himself in the head?' I didn't give a shit about myself at this point, but I couldn't do that to my mother. I just broke down. I just started crying, and then my mom and my stepdad, they found me. I had the gun in my hands. I was so distraught I couldn't even talk.

"I went to a psychiatric hospital after that. I went to the VA [Veterans Administration] hospital. The VA's solution was just to put me back on Paxil and add a couple of other things. At this point, I'm so out of it that I was just believing anything they said. They told me I have major depressive disorder, that I have to take the medicine for the rest of my life. I have to, or I'll probably end up killing myself. This is my only option. I took it and for the next twelve years, it was this horrible cycle of taking the antidepressants that they prescribed me, and then having either horrible side effects, or just horrible negative reactions to the medicine, or the medicine just stopped working. Then, they would have to switch my dose, switch what I'm on, change the dose, increase the dose, add something else.

"Each time this happened, it was a nightmare. It's like a roller coaster with my emotions. I was in and out of the psychiatric hospital. I couldn't keep a job. I didn't have a girlfriend. I was just completely messed up. Then, they put me on Lexapro, which made it to where I couldn't sleep.

"I drank myself to sleep every night, so then I had to drink a little bit more, a little bit more, a little bit more. Then, I got to the point where I was drinking a bottle and a half of vodka every day, just to function. At the same time, I just wanted to die. I didn't have the guts to kill myself, but I just wanted to die, so I was taking twenty-five Lorcets a day, these painkillers. I would take Xanax every day. I was doing coke. I was smoking weed. I would do every drug I could possibly get my hands on. I attempted to overdose a few times. There was one time where I took a whole month's worth of Ativan and then drank some Wild Turkey whiskey, which should have done the trick. It should have killed me, but I woke up from that.

"That was my third suicide attempt, but something happened that time where I realized that I can't even kill myself. Some voice in my head, or something, told me, 'Maybe you're here for a reason.'

"Then, I was thirty years old. I decided to fight. I decided that I wanted to get off all these drugs. I decided I wanted to stop drinking. I decided that I wanted to get my life back. I put myself in rehab. It was a ninety-day program, but I was a really bad case, so they kept me there for eight months. When I got out, I was clean of alcohol. I was clean of [street] drugs, but I was still on the drugs that the VA had prescribed me. At this point, they had me on the maximum dose of Paxil, the maximum dose of Zoloft, the maximum dose of Trazodone, and six other drugs to counteract the effects to keep my blood pressure right.

"I physically could not function. I was 220 pounds. I was sleeping eighteen hours a day. I couldn't keep a job. I just was a zombie. Over the course of the next two years, against my doctor's advice, I weaned myself off all these drugs. I got a really sensitive scale and I weaned myself off very, very slowly. I decided that the last day that I take antidepressants would be December 21, 2012, because there's this prophecy that [that date would bring] like a new age, and stuff, so I decided that's the day that I'm going to quit.

"I tapered myself off, and I did. I quit. That's the last day of taking antidepressants. During this time, I was taking mushrooms constantly. I would lower my dose of antidepressants and take more mushrooms. The mushrooms were helping me. They were like a life raft. They were helping me to function in society, [but] they didn't get me back to where I wanted to be. I wanted to be happy. I wanted to be like other people.

"I had read about ayahuasca when I was a kid. I was fascinated with the Amazon rain forest, and I read about the plant medicines. One of the plant medicines is ayahuasca, so I decided that I'm going to go to an ayahuasca retreat. The one that I wanted to go to was way too expensive. It was way out of my range. I got disheartened about it. I had no money in the bank. I was functioning, but I was working only three days a week. I had fifty dollars in my bank account, so I had no idea how I was going to buy a plane ticket to Peru and pay for one of these retreats. Then, I got rear-ended in my truck, and I got some money from the insurance to fix my truck, but I didn't fix my truck. I decided I need fixing more than my truck did. I took this money and I bought a ticket to Peru. I booked a trip with Pulse Tours, with Dan's company.

"The way that I found it was through researching online,

just looking at every resource that I could find, all the review sites. I saw that Pulse Tours had five-star reviews from more than 95 percent of the people who had been there. It was affordable to me. I thought it was too good to be true for them to have so many reviews, and I had heard all these things about ayahuasca, like one session with ayahuasca could be like ten years of psychotherapy. I also heard it connects you with plant spirits and things like that. I didn't really believe any of that stuff, but I had no choice because at this point, I was at the end of my line. I was thirty-five years old, and I was done with this life. I was done being miserable. I just couldn't take it anymore.

"I booked a trip through Pulse Tours. I told my mother that if this doesn't work, I'm hanging myself when I get back. I'm done. If ayahuasca doesn't help me, then I'm hanging myself. That's the way it is. I went down there. I was there for a week, initially, but just that first week was all I needed. The week was the hardest week of my entire life. The first three ceremonies were the hardest things I've ever done, but during that time, somehow, I released my depression. It left me. Then, after the last ceremony, I was happier than I had ever been, the day I was born. I had never been that happy my entire life.

"I go back home. My friends, my family, my coworkers, all these people are like, 'What the hell happened to you? Who are you? Where did you come from?' I'm happy. All of a sudden, I'm happy. Now, in my work place, I'm known as the happiest person. There's this one hostess who works there, she didn't know me before. She told me the other day that I'm the happiest person she's ever met in her life. I was like, 'Wow, if you only fucking knew what it took to get here.'

"Yeah, one week with this plant medicine of ayahuasca cured me of depression. It cured me. It did what twelve years of antidepressants couldn't do. In fact, the antidepressants made my life worse.

"They really made my depression worse. The modern medicine, the American medicine, Veterans Administration medicine, this is all they had to offer. They don't believe in psychedelic plants. They don't believe in using mushrooms, or ayahuasca, or anything like that. The next thing for me, according to them, would have been electrotherapy or who knows what. I don't even want to know what, but luckily, I didn't have to go there.

"It didn't work right away. After the first ceremony, I thought, *What the fuck have I done with myself?* I felt crazier than ever before. I felt worse after the first ceremony. I thought I had damaged my brain. I thought that I'm going to be crazier than ever before, and this was a horrible decision. I really did not want to drink it again, but the staff there really did a great job, especially this guy named Rafa.

"He sat with me all day long, telling me, 'They don't call this work for nothing. It's not easy. It's not a magic pill that you take and then you're happy. I'm sorry, but that's not the way that ayahuasca works. You have to do the work. You've been through a lot. You've been through twelve years of antidepressants. It's changed your brain chemistry. You've been through all sorts of trauma, and all sorts of trouble in your life, and it's just not possible for someone who's been through as much as you to get through it all in one night, even with ayahuasca. You have to keep doing it. Why did you come down here? Remember why you came down here. Dig down deep and do it. You didn't come down here to skip a day of drinking. You came down here for the medicine, and if you don't drink it, it's not going to work. So do you want to be depressed forever, or do you want a way out?' He encouraged me to take it again.

"The second time, I only took one quarter of a dose, and it was still overwhelming. Then, the third time, I took half a dose. It was overwhelming every night. The first three nights were, actually, all four nights, were overwhelming. It felt like way too much. After the third ceremony, I finally felt a little bit happy. I felt happier than I've been since high school, and then after the final ceremony, the fourth ceremony of the week, I felt happier than I ever did since the day I was born. I'm still happier than I've ever been.

"I've gone back and drank it a few times. I've actually [had] it seventeen times, so far, total. All but three of those times have been at Pulse Tours. I did drink it one time in the States, which technically, that's illegal, but there are people who bring it around and lead ceremonies inside the United States. That was a beautiful experience, but I didn't feel like it was as powerful as it was drinking it in the jungle. Whenever we drank it in the jungle, we were drinking it with Shipibo shamans, shamans from the Shipibo tribe. The three shamans at Pulse Tours have a total of sixty-six years—or sixty-eight years, something like that—experience between them. They've seen all sorts of problems. They sing during the whole ceremony. They sing songs in Shipibo, the native language, which I can't understand a word that they're saying, but there's something about the ceremony, something about the songs they sing, something about the experience they bring to the table that really makes the whole thing way more powerful.

"Drinking the medicine, drinking the ayahuasca just on its own, if you just did that by yourself, I think that would be a horrible idea. That could be disastrous. If you just did it on your own, you could end up worse off than you were before, but at Pulse Tours, not only do they have a team of native shamans, and you're doing it in the jungle. You're doing it in the place where it came from. That has to be a factor as well. I can't explain what that means, or why that is a factor, but it is. It was to me, at least. Being in the place where this medicine came from, it let me connect with it that much deeper.

"Not only do they have amazing shamans there, they also have an amazing team of facilitators—the facilitators who speak English who helped me walk back and forth to the bathroom, who helped me when I was crying, who helped me when I was throwing up so bad I thought I couldn't breathe. These guys were my heroes. There's a guy named Ian. There's Ian, and Rafa, and Melissa, these three were my heroes during this time. They played such a huge role, and they've become lifelong friends. We stay in close contact. I actually got a chance to get back. I worked as a facilitator there for three weeks.

"When I was first there, Tatyana, I'm not sure what her title is, but she runs the place, it seems. She told me the first time I was there, she pulled me aside and said, 'Randy, you know you have what it takes to do this kind of work, don't you?' I was like, 'What do you mean?' She said, 'You know you have what it takes to help other people, help other people through this. You've been through so much yourself. Most of the people who are coming here haven't been through half of what you've been through. That's strength. Don't you know that that's a strength? The fact that you got through all that, you're strong. You can help other people now.' She said, 'Would you be interested in working here?' At first, I said, 'Hell no. No way. Absolutely not. This is all too much for me.'

"We kept in touch, and then Ian went on vacation, so they offered me, this time, to work there. Come back and work as a facilitator. It's been the most amazing experience of my entire life.

"There was something amazing that happened while I was down there. I don't know. Time will tell. I am going to help other people. I'm not sure how it's going to be. I'm not sure if it's going to be in ayahuasca ceremonies. I think I'll probably do that more. I don't think I see myself doing that as a full-time profession, but something happened when I was there [last time] that just makes everything that I've been through in my entire life worth it. I met the woman of my dreams, literally. I had dreamed about her a month before I left for the jungle. I had a dream that I was going to meet a Russian woman. I saw the color of her hair. I saw her in my dream. I saw everything but her face. I couldn't see her face very clearly, but I knew she was a Russian woman. I even had a feeling that she was from the same area as Tatyana. As it turns out, she was born in the same city as Tatyana. We are just completely head over heels in love with each other.

"The thing is, she lives in Dubai, so I'm going to go to Dubai, long enough to look for a job while I'm there. We want to move in with each other. It's crazy, but it's like a fairy tale. It's amazing. Also, she had dreams of me. She told me that she's been dreaming of me since she was a little girl. I was lonely for ten years. For ten years, I've been single with no luck with relationships. As a facilitator, they give us one night off per week for us to drink the medicine, for us to do our own work. My intention for that night, that I drank, the week that she was there, was asking the medicine to please help me understand why I've had bad luck with relationships for ten years, why I've been single for ten years. The message I got was, 'Go to Mikayla.' I got a message as clear as day, 'Leave your past in the maloca.' The maloca is the ceremonial space. 'Leave your past in the maloca and go to Mikayla.' I literally crawled over there to her mat, and we fell in love at an ayahuasca ceremony.

"People ask me what has changed, and I have to say, 'Everything.'

"Before I went down there, I had a good job, but I was working only three days a week, and I was just getting by. I was just paying the bills. Also, I was smoking weed still. I still had that habit. I figured as soon as I get back home, the first thing I'm going to do is smoke weed, go roll up a joint and smoke it, and celebrate as soon as I get home. Actually, the first thing I did was I went, I picked it all up—I picked up my pipe, my weed, my paraphernalia, everything—took it straight to the trash, and threw it away. I said, 'I don't need this anymore.'

"[When] I was working three days a week, I was a mediocre employee at my job, but since I've come back, now I work five days a week, even six days a week sometimes, and I enjoy it. I do it because I want to. I'm making more money than I need, so I'm saving money, which allows me to do things, like take a month off to go to the jungle and buy tickets to Dubai, take almost a month off while

I look for a job in Dubai. All these things are falling into place because I like working. When I came home from the first retreat, when I got on the airplane, I thought, *Wow, I've never been so happy to get on the airplane.* When I got home, I thought, *Wow, I've never been so happy to get home.* When I did laundry, I was like, 'I've never been so happy to do laundry.'

"Everything was better. Everything. Everything across the whole board. Even the problems that my family had, everybody has problems in their family, but the problems that my family members had, they didn't bother me anymore. In fact, I can help them. I help them through a lot now. They lean on me. I'm like the healer in the family now. Whenever there's a problem, they come and they ask me for my perspective. They want to know, so my whole life has changed. Everything has changed.

"My mom and my two sisters, they were supportive. [My mom] already knew that I didn't want to live anymore, and this was my last resort, ayahuasca. My father was not so supportive. My parents got divorced when I was little, but my biological father was not so supportive because he's a deacon of the Baptist church. He thought, *Oh, you're going to go to do drugs in a hippie camp in the jungle. That's not going to help you with anything.* My family talked to him and said, 'Look, Randy's going to do this, whether you like it or not. He's already bought the ticket. He's already paid for it. He's going. You might as well support your son.

This is your only son. He feels like he needs to do this, so you might as well be behind him.' So he reluctantly gave his blessing—very reluctantly.

"He took me to the airport for my first trip. Even on the ride to the airport, he told me, 'I don't think you should be doing this. You just need to go to church, and find a woman in church, and then you'll be happy.' I was like, 'No, you don't fucking understand. You don't even know your own son. You're so wrapped up in all that church stuff that you don't even know me anymore, never really have.' But when I came home, he also was the one to pick me up from the airport, and he was shocked. He was shocked. He was like, 'Are you still high? Are you OK?' I'm like, 'No, I'm not high on anything. I'm completely sober, but I've never been happier in my life.'

"It took him a while. It took him a few days to even believe it, but after a couple of weeks back home, I went to lunch with him and he said, 'Randy, I want to tell you something. I really see a huge change in you, before and after you go into the jungle. I just want to tell you, any time you feel like you need to do that, go ahead and do it.' He said he's not claiming to understand it. He's definitely not going to go to the jungle and drink ayahuasca himself, ever, but he's glad that I did it."

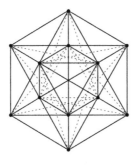

CHAPTER SEVEN

MORE LESSONS FROM THE JUNGLE (REAL AND METAPHORICAL)

CHOOSE YOUR PARTNERS WELL

I now know that I have to give 100 percent to any venture I undertake, but I also know that I cannot do it alone. I need to work with partners I can trust for the long term.

Going into business with someone is a little like getting married. You hope your common ground will serve you well, but you should also be prepared for conflict. My father likes to say that every partnership ends in divorce, so it's best to begin with the end in mind. Going into a partnership, everything may look great: you enjoy a friendly relationship and each brings complementary talents, skills, and investment goals to the enterprise. Still, you don't know how the picture might change down the road. The best thing you can do is make sure you really know your prospective partners before you commit.

My best advice is to have a strong partnership agreement in place before you start anything. This is advice I wish I had taken with my kratom venture. Set out expectations for each player. What will each partner contribute? What percentage will he or she own? How will he or she exit the business? Everybody is hopeful at the beginning; it's human nature to be optimistic about scenarios turning out exactly how we want them, but it doesn't always go as planned. Prepare for turbulence. Eventually, somebody is going to want out or the business will need to be sold. If you have the details of dissolution spelled out from the beginning, it can save a lot of agony and heartbreak when situations change.

Another aspect of relationships to consider is how they reflect on you, your reputation, and your brand. I adhere to Robert Greene's rule from *48 Laws of Power*: protect your reputation with your life. Simply by association, the folks you do business with reflect on you. That includes employees. At Pulse Tours and Ayahuasca Adventure Center, we need to hire impeccable staff because they affect our guests' experience and it's our guests who ultimately determine our reputation and our brand.

As Bruce Poon Tip says in his book, *The Looptail*, your brand is what people say about you when you're not in the room. It's not about what you say or how you promote yourself; it's about what others say about you through reviews, testimonials, social media, and plain-old word of mouth.

Early on, we hit some stumbling blocks with our relationships. We depended too heavily on Manuel's lodge, for instance, without preparing for the possibility that he wouldn't always have our best interests at heart. His unreliable reservation system could have killed us before we even got started. The people you work with need to understand that it's your reputation on the line, too.

As you become more successful, your activities become more visible, so it's even more crucial to choose partners with the utmost integrity. I learned a lot about this from Aubrey Marcus of Onnit, who works only with people who have impeccable reputations. For him to put his stamp of approval on someone else's product or process, he has to be 110 percent certain that the person he is associating his name with is going to respect that honor.

Relationships work both ways, of course. That's why it's equally important to approach your business transactions from a place of honesty and honor. If you develop your reputation as a trustworthy person, other trustworthy people are going to want to do business with you.

I am still a novice in a lot of areas of business. I don't

have the slightest clue, for instance, how to run a *Fortune 500* company. Maybe that is something I will someday be doing, but I am going to take it step by step. I know that the only way to truly internalize the lessons needed is through practice and experience.

LUCKY CHARMS

As much as I would like to take credit for all the success Pulse Tours and Ayahuasca Adventure Center has had, I acknowledge that luck played a huge role in how the business grew. Several lucky breaks moved us further down the road than expected, like the pivotal 2013 Reddit post. Doing an "Ask Me Anything" (AMA) segment was just something a good friend suggested to me in passing, not anything recommended by the marketing gurus. Learning that such an opportunity even existed was completely serendipitous; if my friend hadn't mentioned it, I would never have thought of it. And yet, the response to that AMA Q & A session propelled us to a new level and continued to feed us leads for years afterward.

The second lucky break I got was meeting Tatyana. She brightened my outlook and brought a much-needed feminine energy to my life and the business. It felt so good to not be alone anymore. Now I had a partner, and the business was our joint project. We never would have met without that first contact on Facebook; we wouldn't have known about each other at all. Our personal relationship, and all the skills Tatyana has brought to the center—she's been a salesperson, a tour leader, and a facilitator, and is now learning the medicine itself—would never have transpired without that first note.

Finding AyaAdvisors.org and the Joe Rogan podcast early on was the third piece of luck that sent us on our way. We found the site before it was overly popular, so we were able to position ourselves at the top of the reviews list. Then Amber Lyon mentioned AyaAdvisors.org on Joe Rogan's show, and we were suddenly the first company anyone seeking an ayahuasca experience considered.

It's true you have to do your due diligence. You have to strategize, plan, and execute things like search engine optimization and so on. However, for our particular situation, it was these three lucky moments that were essential to the speed and amplitude of our growth.

The story I am telling here is not so much about how I am such a great entrepreneur but about all the things that went into making the Pulse venture work. Author Ryan Holiday warns in his book *Ego Is the Enemy* that entrepreneur authors can sometimes give themselves all the credit, when that's almost never the truth. "I did it and here's how" is not an honest narrative because it doesn't take into account the fact that lucky breaks really matter. Without lucky breaks, our business would not be alive today.

People ask me if it was really luck or fate at work. I'm

a pragmatic person, so I don't often put circumstances in a spiritual context. At the same time, I sometimes think that I was given a second lease on life after my fall because I was meant to do this. Maybe I created what I was put here to create. I don't pretend to know; fate could be a factor, or it could be just a string of unrelated events that intersected to create this outcome. I'm open to both ideas.

EVERYTHING ECHOES

Whether or not fate is involved, there is certainly an element of karma in business. There are always consequences; what you do in business with others will impact what happens in your business. That's a concept I learned from Bruce Poon Tip at G Adventures: everything echoes. If you take advantage of people or fail to take care of them, others may do the same to you. If you're contributing to the welfare of others, looking after your customers, employees, and community, on the other hand, that will keep the fires that fuel your business fully stoked.

I'm somewhat reticent to accept the concept of karma as a universal force; I feel like it's something that happens internally. If you wrong somebody, you know it, and that energy influences your perceptions and decisions. For me, it might manifest in some sort of self-sabotage in the future. But if I'm constantly doing good things and living up to my promises, I may feel more deserving and so open up to the good things that come my way.

The way this works on a practical level at Pulse Tours and Ayahuasca Adventure Center is that we work hard to live up to our word. For example, we make good on our promises to the villagers who work with us and for us. Taking care of people and supporting the community comes back to us several times over in the form of honest, dedicated employees who love working with us and want to see us succeed. We have developed a family environment, where everyone has everyone else's back, so nobody feels overlooked or unappreciated. Everyone is working for the greater good of all.

Clients who come and spend time with us sense the community spirit we have built. They feel comfortable and know they are in good hands. That, in turn, gives them a positive customer experience, which results in referrals and return guests for us.

Reviews and referrals are the lifeblood of our business. If we ever receive less than stellar feedback, we try to make it right as quickly and fairly as possible. Early on, we received a negative review that was devastating to us. We immediately promised to give the client a full refund. It turned out that this guest was wildly exaggerating the problems he had on his retreat, but we nonetheless refunded his fee because we had promised him that we would.

We probably spent too much energy defending ourselves from what grew into an overblown Internet attack, and the more we protested, the worse we looked. We decided to approach it differently, and looked at what our role was in the problem. Was our staff experienced enough? Were Tatyana and I spending enough time on-site? Did we have enough hands on deck? What could we do, going forward, that would make a positive difference?

Putting energy into growth and learning paid off. I would say that 99 percent of the people who spend time at our center are happy with their experience. Ninety percent are over-the-moon happy; their lives are changed. Probably about 9 percent have a positive, but not necessarily transformative, experience. There will always be the remaining 1 percent who don't enjoy their stay. The jungle is not for everyone. On the other hand, the people who love us really love us, as we can see reflected in the personal stories told throughout this book.

MENTORS AND TEACHERS

As much as luck and intention are important factors for success in business, so is having a network of people who can help you along the way. When I've been unsure of which path to take, people like my father, Tatyana, Carlos, and other entrepreneurs have shared their wisdom and helped me gain perspective.

FAMILY AND FRIENDS

My father can check me like nobody else. He knows me better than I know myself sometimes. When I'm stuck in moments of frustration and itching to just get out of the business altogether, my father understands that I need to shift my perspective to the long term. He talks me out of giving up and sets me on the path to growth and improvement instead. Or when I have a harebrained scheme for a new life-move that I think is brilliant, he might remind me of critical information that I sometimes overlook when enamored with a new idea.

Tatyana is always the voice of reason, not only contributing her efforts to the organization, but also her calm demeanor and wholehearted approach to life. I can get trapped in my thoughts, but Tatyana brings me back to my emotions. I often allow her to talk sense into me, when I'm coming from a place of intellect or ego, instead of from a place of heart.

ALL HANDS ON DECK

All of the people who work for Pulse are crucial as well, whether it's the facilitators who are driving the ceremonies and making sure people are taken care of and safe or the shamans who have put their hearts and souls into healing people. Folks like Carlos make the whole enterprise possible, managing details and maintenance and relationships with the village. Our jungle guides offer indispensable expertise when they take our guests out into nature. The list of people who guide this business is long, and I am grateful to them all.

The biggest mistake entrepreneurs can make is to assume that they can go out and do it on their own. That's ego talking; it's utterly unfeasible. That's how failures happen. You have to engage other people, build your network, and inspire other people to want to work with you. The principle of reciprocity works: take care of other people and they take care of you.

STORIES OF PERSONAL TRANSFORMATION:
MELISSA STANGL

Melissa Stangl is the director of operations at Pulse Tours and Ayahuasca Adventure Center. She has a background in engineering, science, and management. At Pulse, Melissa helps keep the ship running smoothly. She also organizes and leads monthly tours to Machu Picchu and the Sacred Valley. Here, she talks about how she broke out of the corporate world and into a much richer way of life.

"About three years ago now, a little bit more, I was just graduating from college in Philadelphia and I was studying bioengineering. I had a lot of student debt and I was looking for a job. I ended up taking a job that was operations management for an industrial supply company. I had a little bit of time between graduating college and starting this job. I had a feeling that I wasn't going to love this job. I basically took it for the money. It was very much a corporate America-type position. It was their management development program. I had a little bit of time in between starting that job and I wanted to go on a trip or do something exciting before I entered this next phase of my life.

"I was looking around on Reddit and found an aya-huasca forum. I had been following that for a little while at that point. My interest in consciousness and psychedelics blossomed toward the end of my college years. One day, I was looking at that and there was a post from Dan [Cleland]; he was basically just doing these tours on his own around South America. He was advertising for a June solstice journey, which was basically to take people to do ayahuasca ceremonies, as well as an adventure tour all around South America, Peru, and a little bit of Colombia as well.

"Perfect timing for me. It was right before I was about to start the job, and because I had discovered ayahuasca, I had an interest in it. I talked to him and connected with him and asked him a bunch of questions and read through the whole post. He seemed very personable. He answered everybody's questions. He answered all my questions. He seemed like a really great guy, so I was interested in doing it.

"At the time I was dating somebody and he was very skeptical that I was going to go all the way to Peru to the jungle to do ayahuasca with somebody I had met on Reddit; so was my whole family. I just had a really good feeling about it. I felt like Dan was a good guy. It was a perfect timing in my life. I really wanted to do it. I ended up saying to my boyfriend at the time, 'I'm going to go do this. I really want to do this. If you're so worried about it, come with me.'

"He did end up coming with me, and we were a bit nervous right before it happened, but we basically flew into Peru and we were like, 'OK, I hope somebody has a sign with our name on it when we get out of the plane.' Sure enough, they did, and we met up with the group. We were actually the last two people to join the group that evening, and they were in Bogotá, Colombia. We met the group and it was an amazing trip. It was an amazing group. Everything went very, very smoothly. It was actually the trip that Dan and Tatyana met on. Tatyana came as a guest then, but she also had helped coordinate a little bit.

"We traveled through Bogotá, Leticia, to Iquitos; the first half of the trip was just purely jungle adventures and tours. Then the last half was through another ayahuasca center doing ceremonies. The whole trip was just super-smooth and organized extremely well. It was a pretty large group of us and it was Dan's first trip where he was branching outside of friends and family to run the tour. It was a really successful trip and it was perfect for me before I went back into corporate America.

"At the end of the trip, I told Dan, 'I've got to go take this job, but I really, really like what you're doing here. I'd love to stay in touch.' After that trip, Dan and Tatyana had fallen in love and they decided to go full time with the company from there and start doing tours full time and see where that took them. I was of course really, really happy. We were all excited that they got together. Then I said, 'I'd love to keep in touch.' I went back home and I took the job and I hated it exactly as much as I thought I would.

"Over the next year I kept in touch with Dan and followed his progress doing more tours and in the next year he and Tatyana wanted to build a center of their own as they were getting a little too big for the center they were working through. At that point, I offered my services again to help Dan in writing a business plan to build the center. We worked together a little bit on that as well. Not quite positive if he ever actually used it, but it was one of those things that I just wanted to offer my help and services and stay connected to his progress while I still was working in America.

"He ended up building the center, and then over the next year we lost touch a little bit, but I followed his progress and watched the center grow and blossom. Then a year after that, I was very much ready to be out of the job I was in. I had already been looking for other positions but hadn't found anything I was very passionate about. This was about May of last year, of 2015. I was thinking of moving, and then all of the sudden one day, I get this e-mail from Dan and Tatyana, as an e-mail blast, saying, 'Hey, we're expanding our team and we need an operations manager as one of the positions.' I got really excited because that was exactly what I was doing in my current position. I don't like applying for jobs. I don't like writing cover letters, all these things. With this position, I thought, *I have to at least try. I don't think I'm going to get it, but I have to try.* It was the easiest application I had ever written. It came so quickly and smoothly.

"I submitted it and crossed my fingers and then got a message a few days later from Dan saying, 'I got your application. Thank you for it. Just a couple questions. Do you understand that this involves at least a one-year relocation to Iquitos, Peru, and do you think that you can get your Spanish good enough in the next few months to talk with fast-talking, slang-using Peruvians?' I said, 'Yes, I know this involves relocation.' And then I said, 'Give me a few months and I'll be able to...I'll learn Spanish, basically. What I'm doing now is operations management, so if you can pay me, I'd love to do it there.' He offered me the job and I was like, 'OK, now that I got the job, I have to take it.'

"It was a really cool transition to [escape] from corporate America, selling all my stuff. I sold my car, ended my relationship, packed everything up, and moved down here. It's been the best decision I've ever made in my life. I'm so grateful to these guys for allowing me onto their team, and I've been able to carve out a little niche for myself here and keep things running smoothly. It's one of those things that I constantly marvel at the fact that my intuition's saying, 'I have a good feeling about this,' three years ago has led me to where I am today. That's pretty exciting.

"If I had any idea what the good feeling really meant three years ago, I wouldn't have even believed it, honestly. Now I can't imagine doing anything else.

"I drink [ayahuasca] about once or twice a week now. It's up to my discretion as long as I do my job, get my work done. I'm not a facilitator during ceremonies, so I just coordinate everything behind the scenes. I can drink pretty much whenever I want to.

"I'm really, really lucky to be able to work long term with a medicine like this. It's truly made me a whole different person. I'm so much happier now, in a much better way, and I feel as though I'm really progressing on a personal level. Working with this medicine long term, I'm able to help others who come through as well on their journey.

"I feel like I'm in a unique position because I come from the science world and I did engineering and come from very Western thinking. I have trouble breaking out of those boxes, even now, but it's actually a good thing because my skepticism and the newness toward the spiritual world is actually helpful for relating to a lot of guests who come through who have similar backgrounds as I do. I have one foot in each world and I can sometimes act as a bit of a bridge to help people trust in the process a little bit more, trust in the medicine, and then really get the most that they can out of it.

"The thing that I hear most often, [from] people who come through here, is just immediately how comfortable and safe they feel. I really like the way that we do the group setups. A lot of other centers have a setup where you can come start with them at any point and end at any point.

You have people overlapping some days but not others and starting and finishing all at different times. The way that we do things is basically a week-by-week group. You're with the same people for the entire week, and I found that that really facilitates some pretty amazing bonding experiences for the group throughout the week because by the end of the week, they're a real family, a real unit.

"I've heard a lot of people say, 'I come here and I meet fifteen people who are as open-minded as I am and I go back home and I don't have any of those connections.' How quickly they form the connections, and then the fact that they're with the same people for the whole week facilitates a really profound healing process. I think that's a huge part of this work with the medicine. I like the way that we do that. I feel as though people immediately get a sense of family when they come with us. I definitely think that sets us apart a little bit and forms lifelong friendships and connections that people can turn to after they go home.

"Beyond that as well, I like that we've got a setup that involves a little bit more adventure and seeing more of the Amazon and remaining active to help in the process of healing as well. Fun is a big part of it, and also, I think the family-bonding aspect of it is definitely unique for Pulse.

"I thought I was maybe going to be a lab rat for a while or something like that or stuck in the corporate rut. It's amazing. I feel very fortunate to have found something I'm truly passionate about. I will always be grateful to Dan and Tatyana and to myself for finally listening to my own intuition and pursuing myself and my dreams."

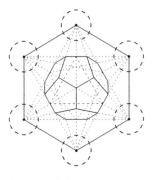

CHAPTER EIGHT

PARTING ADVICE AND CALL TO ACTION

I HAVE LEARNED A GREAT DEAL FROM ENTREPRE-
neurial thought leaders and I'd like to share some of that
with those reading this book and looking forward to their
own entrepreneurial pursuits.

One guiding principle I gleaned from Tim Ferriss was
this: focus on results rather than work. By applying the
80/20 rule, I found that Ferriss is right that you can get 80
percent of the results for 20 percent of the effort. Perfec-
tionism can stall your progress; if you are unable to move
forward until you reach 100 percent perfection, you may
never move forward. Plus, you'll put a lot more work into
making that 20 percent materialize. Ferriss showed me
that you don't have to do all of that yourself. He talks about

putting outsourcing, automation, and efficiency to work for you. That's what I try to do in the day-to-day operation of Pulse Tours and Ayahuasca Adventure Center.

There's an obsession in North America with the forty-to-eighty-hour work week that I've never bought into, although I started out in Canada. Even in my early sales days, I aimed at establishing a few big accounts rather than collecting a number of small accounts. The profit from either strategy was the same, but fewer accounts means less work. I was living with guys who worked in the trades at the time, though, who didn't understand my philosophy. They wanted to know why I didn't get a "real job." I saw them getting up at six o'clock in the morning and going to work in rain or shine, and I wasn't interested.

The Puritan work ethic is ingrained in the North American culture. Puritans found God through hard work. It served their religious beliefs. We don't necessarily need that today, though. By applying the principles Ferriss lays out in *The 4-Hour Workweek*, we can get more out of what we do and focus on the key performance indicators. It requires a mental paradigm shift, a focus on high-leverage activities, but there are ways to get excellent results without necessarily putting in a ridiculous amount of work.

Our question shouldn't be, "How can I fill up forty hours?" It should be, "How can I get forty hours' worth of work done in twenty hours?" Think about the average North American worker. A salaried job may require him or her to put in forty hours a week. What if he or she finds a way to get all of his or her work done in twenty hours? The company doesn't give him or her twenty hours off. Instead, he or she may get more work. Many workers end up working inefficiently just to fill up their time. It seems backward to me.

Endlessly filling the hours with work means we don't have time or energy to devote to things that are meaningful to us. This was my experience with the kratom company I started. On a basic level, I was unhappy with the business because I wasn't doing the world any good with that company. I was just capitalizing on an opportunity and then maintaining the daily grind necessary to push out the product.

When it came time to make a choice between the kratom business and Pulse Tours, Pulse always won. That's where my purpose was. When you have work that is intrinsically satisfying, you might have a little bit less money at the end of the day, but because you are happier, you don't need to fill a void by spending money on instant gratification. You're already gratified.

When you choose a profession or a project, it's important to pursue something that provides intrinsic value. Build on ideas you believe in, activities that you know are going to make you feel good at the end of the day. The emotional and psychological rewards are a much more effective motivator than just chasing the dollar.

From reading this book, you can see that meaningful doesn't necessarily mean easy. It was a long road to success for Pulse Tours and Ayahuasca Adventure Center. But if I can come back from rock bottom to feeling like I'm on top of the world, you can, too.

FURTHER READING

Belsky, Scott. *Making Ideas Happen: Overcoming the Obstacles between Vision and Reality.* New York: Penguin/Portfolio, 2010.

Ferris, Timothy. *The 4-Hour Workweek.* New York: Random House, 2009.

Greene, Robert. *The 48 Laws of Power.* New York: Penguin, 2000.

Hofstede, Geert. *Culture's Consequences: Comparing Values, Behaviors, Institutions and Organizations across Nations.* New York: Sage, 2003.

Holiday, Ryan. *Ego Is the Enemy*. New York: Penguin/Portfolio, 2016.

McKenna, Dennis. "Clinical Investigations of the Therapeutic Potential of Ayahuasca: Rationale and Regulatory Challenges." *Pharmacology and Therapeutics* 102 (2004): 111–129.

Poon Tip, Bruce. *The Looptail: How One Company Changed the World by Reinventing Business*. New York: Business Plus, 2013.

Sanders, Michael. *Ayahuasca: An Executive's Enlightenment*. Toronto: Sage and Feather Press, 2015.

Sinek, Simon. *Start with Why: How Great Leaders Inspire Everyone to Take Action*. New York: Penguin/Portfolio, 2009.

Tylor, Edward Burnett. *Primitive Culture and Anthropology*. New York: Torchbooks, 1958.

Warner, Brad. *Sit Down and Shut Up: Punk Rock Commentaries on Buddha, God, Truth, Sex, Death*. Novato, CA: New World Library, 2007.

ACKNOWLEDGMENTS

FIRST AND FOREMOST, I MUST GIVE THANKS TO THE team at Book In A Box for taking this book from idea to publication. Sheila Trask, JT McCormick, Dan Bernitt, Holly Hudson, and of course, Tucker Max for founding this incredible company. Thanks also to Aubrey Marcus for making the introduction. The content of this book would not have manifested without an incredible decade of experience wherein I always knew I had a powerhouse of a family behind me if I failed—Mom, Dad, Emily, Meghan, and Catherine. Tatyana, thank you for tolerating me and being my soul-soothing sidekick from the beginning. Thanks to the team at Pulse for delivering the kind of love and positive change the world needs today, and to all the Pulse patrons who've become part of our growing community. Last but not least, thanks to the village of Libertad for allowing us to be part of their community and to build our healing oasis in their little slice of Amazon paradise.

Pulse of the Jungle was brought to life in part with the help of these brave early adopters who stepped up to the plate and preordered multiple copies of the book. Although many more people preordered one to three copies, for whom I'm also eternally grateful, I give special thanks to the following people for their generous contributions to my campaign: Guy Vincent, Brian Wallace, Elizabeth Aber, Chase Anthony, Chris Williams, Bryce Goertzen, Jeffrey Hill, Robert Erwin, Christine Daniero, and Robert Dancer.

ABOUT THE AUTHOR

 DANIEL CLELAND, once a small-town Canadian boy, is today a global social entrepreneur who works all over the world from his home base in the jungles of South America. He is the cofounder of Pulse Tours and Ayahuasca Adventure Center, a spiritual adventure company operating in places like Peru, Colombia, and Brazil. His Ayahuasca Adventure Center, a spiritual healing center located at the 2.2 million-hectare Pacaya-Samiria reserve near Iquitos, Peru, offers people from all walks of life a way to integrate, expand, and transform the human experience on multiple levels. Informed by more than a decade of adventure tour leadership, corporate sales experience, and a Master of Arts degree in Intercultural and International Communication from Royal Roads University, Dan builds strong intercultural bridges between travelers and locals, as well as a clear pathway to personal—and often professional—fulfillment through his programs.